# INCLUSION

## THE COMMON CORE CURRICULUM AND THE HIGH STAKES TESTS

BOOSTING THE OUTCOMES FOR STRUGGLING LEARNERS, GRADES 5-12

## Sonya Heineman Kunkel

HEINEMAN PRESS
CROMWELL, CT
2013

Inclusion, the Common Core Curriculum and the High Stakes Tests: Boosting the Outcomes for Struggling Learners, Grades 5-12 / Sonya Heineman Kunkel

-1st ed.
Includes index

ISBN-13: 978-1480172715
ISBN-10: 1480172715

**For additional materials, including the new co-teaching APP for android smart phones, as well as resources, coaching or professional development opportunities, contact Sonya Heineman Kunkel www.KunkelConsultingServices.com**

This book is dedicated to Mom and Dad.

As a professional artist and art teacher, Luciana Heineman taught me anyone can learn. When I was very young, I accompanied her whenever she taught classes at the local Senior Center. One woman, a stroke victim, wanted to learn how to paint with watercolors despite being paralyzed from the neck down. Mom added a beautiful ribbon to our spaghetti strainer, turning the strainer into a "hat" with a large bow. Then with PVC pipe and duct tape, she attached two different brushes to this helmet. Her student learned to paint by manipulating the brushes with her head.

To Mom:  Thank you for teaching me to be creative and tenacious.

Ernest Heineman escaped from Germany as a young Jewish boy. Despite his wartime struggles to survive, he never lost his sense of humor, his integrity or his patience. A hard-working immigrant, Dad knew that perseverance pays off and that to live well, you must "pay it forward."

To Dad:  Thank you for teaching me to always see the glass as half full...
...because you never know the value of the other half.

# Table of Contents

## Modifying and Understanding the IEP ...... 63

# Introduction

Including struggling learners in the secondary classroom is not always an easy thing to do. However, it can be a tremendously rewarding experience for both students and teachers.

Consider Daniel. When I was just starting out as a high school special education teacher, he was among my students. In the classroom, he was hindered by a learning disability, but on the athletic field, Daniel excelled. He became very frustrated by the difficulty he had with academic learning and decided he would drop out of school. His coach and I drove to his home and persuaded Daniel to stick with it. He was reassured that he would be allowed to learn at his own pace, and that I would never push him beyond his ability.

I tailored my teaching strategies to his learning style, and he responded with genuine dedication. Not only did Daniel regain his self-confidence as a student, he graduated from high school and attended college as well. Daniel now teaches elementary school in the Washington, D.C. area, paying forward his positive learning experience.

As we teach toward educational standards, creativity becomes an essential ingredient if we are to help students with disabilities meet classroom objectives. Successfully including all students requires thinking differently about how to teach the content.

For instance, imagine that you're trying to explain the concept of geometric shapes to a group of tactile learners who have trouble relating to flat lines on a one-dimensional surface. To bring the concept to life for them, you might utilize a simple prop such as a colorful handkerchief. As deftly as a magician, you fold it once to create a rectangle or a triangle. Bunched up, it becomes a sphere. In the everyday world, it's still just a simple piece of cloth; but for those tactile learners, it's an educational tool that can effectively attach real-world meaning to the term "hypotenuse."

Just as a learning strategy can unlock content for students, an easily implemented teaching strategy can unlock the communication barriers that often exist between general education teachers and struggling learners.

This collection of strategies has been successfully implemented in secondary schools, and has been designed to provide students with "supports and services" in the least restrictive environment in accordance with Individuals with Disabilities Education Improvement Act (IDEIA or fka P.L. 94-142). Included are many tips and ideas for supporting our colleagues and ourselves as we move toward the goal of educating all children to their fullest potential.

Daniel was my inspiration for writing this book. My hope is that in sharing some fun and simple teaching strategies, general education teachers will be inspired to reach out to struggling learners like Daniel. I know from experience that the challenge of inclusion can be rewarding for everyone.

-Sonya Heineman Kunkel

# Teacher's Heaven

A teacher died and went to heaven. St. Peter welcomed her in and said that he would show her to her mansion. The first neighborhood was lovely. People were out on park lawns, socializing, grilling or out on a beautiful golf course, playing golf and having a great time.

The teacher asked, "Is this my neighborhood?"

St. Peter replied, "No, this neighborhood is exclusively for doctors."

They walked on, and the teacher saw another neighborhood that was just as beautiful: huge mansions, beautiful grounds, swimming pool and a golf course. The residents were out enjoying themselves and having a great time.

Again the teacher inquired, "Is this my neighborhood?"

St. Peter said, "No, this neighborhood is exclusively for dentists."

On through the clouds they walked, approaching another neighborhood. It, too, was beautiful, with parks and pools and huge mansions. St Peter told her that this was her new home in heaven. The teacher was thrilled, except she noticed that no one was around and that the mansions seemed to be empty.

She asked St Peter, "Where is everyone? Don't teachers make it to heaven?"

St. Peter announced, "Yes, there are lots of teachers in heaven, and they will return tomorrow. Today, they are all in hell attending a staff development day."

Staff development can assume many forms. This book is intended for the individual who is professionally growing through self-study, for a team receiving training from a professional developer such as myself, Sonya Kunkel, for a college professor working with students studying to be teachers, or for the reflective practices often found in professional learning communities.

INCLUSION

# What is Inclusion?

Inclusion is a philosophical belief that all students can be educated in a single environment, even though a wide range of academic diversity may exist. Students with disabilities learn age-appropriate material at levels commensurate with their certified ability.

Quite often, I hear teachers say, "I teach the inclusion class," or "A lot of the special education kids participate in a general education classroom, and I go in and teach the inclusion class." Which begs the question, "What about your colleagues that don't teach the *in*clusion class? Are they teaching the *ex*clusion class?"

## The Difference Between Inclusion and Mainstreaming

Mainstreaming was the first step toward rectifying an arrangement where students with disabilities attended school, but were segregated from and did not interact with the general education students. Mainstreaming required students to be capable of remaining close to the curriculum standard before they were allowed to sit in the general education classroom. Occasionally, a tweak might have been made to the curriculum, but it would not amount to much. For example, a student might have been mainstreamed in gym class or in language arts, but he would still have been relegated to a self-contained math class because math was his area of weakness.

The philosophy behind inclusion is that students have the right to belong in the typical age-appropriate environment with the appropriate supports and services to gain access to the general education standard. That means that they don't necessarily have to be held to the curriculum standard. While we will always teach toward the standard, students needn't be near the standard to have access to the classroom.

## Inclusion is a Civil Rights Issue

Public Law 94-142, which was passed in 1975, is the basis for special education. It states that:

> "...to the maximum extent appropriate, children with disabilities...are educated with children who are non-disabled; and special classes, separate schooling or other removal...from the regular education environment occurs only if...education in regular classes with the use of supplementary aids and services cannot be achieved satisfactorily."

As teachers, we need to provide students with supplementary aids and services in the least restrictive environment (LRE), which has always has been the general education classroom.

Court cases have shaped inclusion, resulting in the requirement to try the LRE, first and foremost, with accommodations, modifications, and specially designed instruction. After a period of time, we have to ask ourselves:

## *"Is the student benefiting academically?"*

This is not the same as asking whether the student is meeting the standards. The second question to be asked is:

## *"Are there any benefits at all to that student being included?"*

Benefits might be social, emotional or vocational. Next, we have to ask:

## *"What are the effects on the rest of the class of that student being included?*

And finally:

## *"What is the cost?"*

Those are the inclusion test questions handed down from the Supreme Court case (Sacramento City School District v. Rachel Holland, 1994).

In the final analysis, we want to include any child with a disability in the general education environment because:

- ➢ There might be some academic benefit for the student

- ➢ There might be a social benefit for the student

- ➢ The effects on the classroom are not beyond the scope of what might occur in a general class

- ➢ It won't break the system financially to have that student in the classroom

Provided the student has no serious behavioral problems and is not negatively affecting the rest of the class, we should view the student as a member of the school community and assume that he or she is capable of making valuable contributions in the classroom.

That's the philosophy behind inclusion.

Is it a legal requirement? No. However, it becomes an option in terms of how we interpret the LRE. In addition, many advocacy groups are promoting this philosophy.

See this resource for additional information on Least Restrictive Environment and Free and appropriate public education:

http://www.wrightslaw.com/info/lre.faqs.inclusion.htm for an article entitled: "Inclusion: Answers to Frequently Asked Questions from the National Education Association"

Also see this reference from the U.S. Dept. of Education OSERS (Office of Special Education and Rehabilitative Services): http://www.wrightslaw.com/info/lre.osers.memo.idea.htm

# Does Inclusion Make a Difference?

In 1999, Spencer J. Salend and Laurel M. Garrick Duhaney published a research article entitled, "The Impact of Inclusion on Students With and Without Disabilities and Their Educators." This was a culminating study that reviewed all of the major inclusion research to measure the effect of the policy on students and teachers.

## Academic benefits

Academic outcomes were compiled from longitudinal studies conducted by the Department of Education in 1995. One very important finding was that for special education students, there was no significant difference in academic progress whether students with a disability were in a general education or a special education classroom. In fact, curriculum-based assessments of students with disabilities in mathematics were higher when the student was taught in general education than if the same student received mathematics instruction in a resource room. That deflates the argument that containment has academic benefits for students with disabilities – or is really the least restrictive environment.

One explanation for why students who were included in general education classrooms scored higher on tests and did better in mathematic skills than in a resource room or than in self-contained mathematics is that the mathematics teacher was teaching toward the standard. General education teachers have to ensure that all of their students are prepared for the high stakes tests. When students with disabilities are confined to a self-contained classroom, the expectations may not be high, and they miss being exposed to the same curriculum standards taught at a rigorous level.

## Effects on the classroom

Salend and Duhaney found that there was:

➢ No significant effect on the amount of time allocated to, or engaged instructional time devoted to, non-disabled peers in classrooms where special education students were included.

➢ No negative effect on the academic performance of non-disabled peers when students with disabilities were included.

## Social outcomes at school

In their research, Salend & Duhaney found that when students with disabilities were included, they:

➢ Had more social interactions

➢ Had larger friendship circles, including more non-disabled peers

➢ Had more lasting relationships with non-disabled peers

## Academic diversity

Academic diversity is not just a pocketed cultural issue; it exists in every school. When we talk about diversity and multi-cultural education, a piece of the puzzle that we often don't include in that education is academic diversity. And yet the research shows that inclusion improves tolerance, which is beneficial to society. When students with disabilities were included:

> - Non-disabled peers were more realistic and positive concerning peers with disabilities.
>
> - Non-disabled peers had greater tolerance and acceptance of differences.

## Benefits beyond high school

What Salend and Duhaney found overwhelmingly was that inclusion had many positive consequences for students with disabilities beyond high school. When these students were not restricted to self-contained classes, they:

> - Attended post secondary education more frequently
>
> - Obtained employment more easily and earned higher salaries
>
> - Lived independently
>
> - Were more integrated in the community
>
> - Were more likely to be engaged and married

## Conclusions

Given that inclusion has significant positive lifelong effects, and containment has no significant benefits, some questions come to mind:

> - Why are we still containing students with disabilities?
>
> - What are the emotional and social advantages of containment beyond high school?

Students who have been contained are less likely to live independently. It would appear that containing students with disabilities is not what's best for all students in the long run.

Recent studies* suggest that inclusive practices should encompass these key areas in order for students and teachers to achieve gains in their scores:

- ❖ *Embedded Instruction and Other Naturalistic Interventions*

- ❖ *Scaffolding Strategies*

- ❖ *Tiered Models of Instruction/Intervention*

- ❖ *Professional Development (PD)*

- ❖ *Models of Collaboration (among professionals)*

- ❖ *Family-Professional Collaboration*

- ❖ *Assistive Technology (AT)*

- ❖ *Universal Design (UD)/Universal Design for Learning (UDL)*

*The National Longitudinal Transition Study*, which is the largest longitudinal study of education outcomes of 11,000 students with disabilities, showed that more time spent in a general education classroom was positively correlated with higher scores on standardized tests of reading and math, fewer absences from school, and fewer referrals for disruptive behavior. These results were independent of students' disability, severity of disability, gender, or socio-economic status (Blackorby, Chorost, Garza, & Guzman, 2003).

Other articles of interest can be found at the National Center on Inclusive Education, a priority area of the University of New Hamphsire Institute on Disability.

http://www.iod.unh.edu/InclusiveEd.aspx

Under the "Resources" tab, select "Research" from the dropdown menu to find an excellent article: *Rationale for and Research on Inclusive Education (Fall 2011)*

# Inclusion Checklist
## Are you ready to include all children?

➢ Do we develop our IEP's based on general education standards?

➢ Do we start by considering the general education classroom with supports and services as the primary option for students with disabilities?

➢ Do we encourage full participation of students with disabilities in all aspects of school life, including extra-curricular?

➢ Are teachers and paraprofessionals trained in current inclusive practices?

➢ Are staff members willing to collaborate in order to make inclusion work?

➢ Are we prepared to support this commitment financially?

➢ Are all staff members willing to take ownership of students with disabilities?

➢ Do special education teachers schedule collaboration time as a top priority before scheduling students?

➢ Do current practices support inclusive outcomes?

➢ Have we defined what "success" is for the students with a disability?

➢ Have we clearly communicated grading procedures?

➢ Have we considered how we will handle issues that may occur with class rank and honor roll?

➢ Do we provide all students with a sense of school community and do we help parents belong to our school community?

➢ Are teachers trained in creating modifications? Do teachers understand their role in modifications and the IEP?

➢ How do we address the child's goals embedded in the general education curriculum?

➢ Are we committed to providing the necessary social supports to promote an inclusive philosophy?

➢ Is our inclusive philosophy aligned with district goals?

Here is an example of a set of beliefs and goals for inclusion for an entire school system. This example was created for a K-12 school system that had no self-contained classrooms or settings. The committee was composed of teachers, parents, and administrators, who all worked collaboratively to provide supports and services in the general education classroom. The goal of the committee was to create opportunities and systemic supports to foster an inclusive philosophy.

<u>Inclusion</u>
East Granby Public Schools
Inclusion Steering Committee

## Statement of Beliefs

*We believe that inclusion is based on the following premises:*

1. Each individual can learn.

2. Each individual is valued.

3. Each individual is accepted for his/her unique abilities and needs.

4. An inclusive school promotes respect for diversity.

5. To the maximum extent possible, students of all abilities are educated with their peers.

## Goals of Inclusion

I.   To celebrate diversity by creating an environment where differences and similarities are taught, learned, accepted and valued.

II.  To schedule all children with a general education teacher in a general education classroom for the greatest amount of time appropriate.

III. To provide all students with an opportunity to participate to their fullest potential as we aim toward meeting district-wide goals.

IV.  To provide appropriate support services to all staff.

V.   To develop a partnership with the community in order to foster collaboration and to support inclusion.

- S. Kunkel and B. D'Amaddio, co-chairs

# Strategies for the Secondary Classroom

## What is a Strategy?

Merriam-Webster's Dictionary defines a strategy as: "The science and art of military command exercised to meet the enemy in combat under advantageous conditions," or "a careful plan or method."

For many of our students, the enemy they meet in combat is the content. They rarely approach tasks with a research-based strategy, but instead use a random pattern. As a result, they're not very successful. A "careful plan or method" is the strategy we teach students to use.

Quite often, we teachers make the mistake of demonstrating a strategy simultaneously with new content. When we do that, the student who has difficulty with processing may not be able to learn a new strategy with new content. Since the content is what students are graded on, they tend to dump the strategy and focus on the content. As a consequence, the student doesn't ever actually master the strategy. By focusing solely on the content, the student with disabilities is left unarmed on the battlefield.

## Strategy-First Instruction

When we teach a new strategy or require students to use a particular approach for managing the curriculum, we must teach the strategy first using mastered materials. Once our data indicates the students have mastered the strategy, we demonstrate to students how the strategy is then applied to new materials. Quite often, it is the material that teachers focus on and <u>not</u> the strategic method. As a result, students with disabilities are lost in the process of how to work with the new material. Once students learn the strategy with new materials, then we must hold them accountable for using the strategy regularly and provide multiple opportunities to practice in and out of the classroom. This will allow the students to become strategically independent.

I'd like to show you what a difference a strategy can make.

> Make a photocopy of the random collection of numbers on page 12.

> Set a timer for one minute. If you need a timer, you can find one online here:

www.online-stopwatch.com

> When the timer starts, try to connect numbers 1 through 60 in numerical order. Start with 1, draw a pencil line to 2, then to 3 and so on.

Ready? Go!

1
34
43
17    52
10
49
6
29
11
55
42    28

27    33
60
19    18  26
2
41
40    48
51    7    12    56
44
35    53    16    32
3    21    30    20

45    25    8    58
15    39  57
24
9    13    54    46    36
38
47    31    37    4
5    59 23    22    50    14

If you're like most people, you didn't get very far. Now take a closer look at the numbers. You may notice that there is a pattern: the odds and the evens are located on opposite sides of the page. When you connect the numbers, you will be creating a zigzag pattern.

With this new information, reset your timer for one minute and try again, starting where you left off.

Ready? Go!

You were probably able to connect many more numbers than during the first attempt. However, there's another piece of information that will unlock the content even further. The zigzag pattern starts at the top of the page and moves down, then moves up again.

With this new information, reset your timer for one minute and try it one more time, beginning where you left off the last time.

Ready? Go!

With this final piece of the puzzle, you were no doubt able to accomplish the task much more efficiently. That is the essence of a strategy: it is an approach that levels the playing field for students who are at a disadvantage.

In the following pages, I'll share some strategies that work well in the secondary classroom.

# Strategies Create Independence

Students with disabilities become independent learners when we teach them strategies for independence, rather than simply offering support.

Strategic instruction is **proactive** and related to each student's goals'. Teachers create a strategic instruction plan through a collaborative process whereby a strategy is targeted that best fits the student's academic demands. By making adult collaboration a priority, strategies can be taught to the level of independent usage by the students, and special education services may be focused in a proactive manner.

For example, if the student has difficulty reading word problems in math and solving the equations, he or she is then taught a very specific strategy to tackle word problems. The student is then expected by the general education and the special education teachers to use the strategy independently on every problem he or she encounters.

Homework help (support) is **reactive** and derives from a lack of proactive collaboration among professionals. By assigning homework that cannot be completed independently, teachers set up a situation where students require assistance and become enabled. It is far more beneficial to collaborate and teach strategies, rather than strand students with homework they do not understand or cannot read because the appropriate planning did not occur.

Many secondary programs for students with mild disabilities only offer classroom support, such as homework help and reteaching. The outcomes of these programs tend to be focused on reactive, wait-to-fail services. Generalized review of high stakes test scores do not show a marked improvement when students receive these types of services. On the other hand, specially designed instruction teaches students specific strategies that they are able to apply independently. This type of proactive service has proven to be much more effective at improving student outcomes.

When we facilitate over a child's shoulder, we begin a pattern of dependence. Students who come through a system where they have been overly supported come to expect ongoing assistance. By teaching strategies that unlock content, we give challenged learners the tools they need to succeed independently.

> Give a kid a fish, you feed him for a day.
>
> Teach a kid to fish, you feed him for a lifetime.

# Memory Strategies

## Chunking

When we break a problem down into manageable parts, that's chunking. We do it all the time with numbers: our phone numbers are broken down into groups of threes and fours, as are our social security numbers. By breaking down a large piece of information into smaller pieces, we can remember it.

## Chunking with a Work folder

A math teacher colleague often employed this strategy. She would break her lesson into thirds and then would visually chunk the materials for students by putting their worksheets in a manila folder with the front cut into thirds. Students would open the top third of the folder, which revealed the first part of the worksheet. After the teacher taught a mini-lesson that lasted 10 to 15 minutes, the students completed the guided practice activities in the first third of the folder. Then she provided a second mini-lesson. After they finished that, they pulled back the second section of the folder so that they could access the second part of the worksheet.

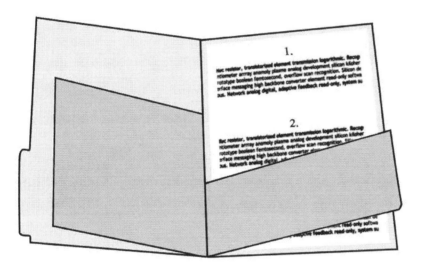

A third mini-lesson was taught and finally, the third section of the folder was pulled back to reveal the last part of the guided practice materials.

For those students that became overwhelmed by large blocks of material, it was a way to chunk it into manageable portions by covering up part of the information.

## Chunking by Drawing a Line

Some students struggle with grapho-motor issues. Without fine motor coordination, it's difficult for them to hold a pen or write on a line. When you use the work folder strategy above, the top edge of the internal sections of the folder provides a writing guide. Another way to achieve this type of "sectioning" would be to draw a line and tell your student, "Don't complete the part below the line until instructed to do so." Or you could use a 3 x 5 card or an envelope as the writing guide (the edge stops the pen). For students with fine motor writing issues, it improves their penmanship. The 3 x 5 card also acts as a visual tracking device.

**Test security: pass out sections in increments**

One frequently asked question pertains to students whose modification includes "extra time" when taking a test. Teachers are often concerned that if the student starts the test in the classroom and then receives the extra time session at a different point in the day, that the student may use the time in between the two sessions to look up answers from the test.

The easiest solution is to divide the test up into sections, each with its own page. Example: section I is on one page, section II on the next page, etc. The student must complete section I before receiving section II. When the child has completed the first two sections and time is up, withhold sections III and IV until the next testing period. When the student comes back for the "extra-time," it lessens the likelihood of a security breach, because the child has not seen sections III or IV until the later session.

**Grouping items by category**

This is another technique you can use in the classroom to facilitate student testing and time usage: group test questions by category. When you do, students aren't forced to switch gears each time they encounter a new subject.

Some years ago, I administered a biology-based final exam to a student by reading the 200 Scantron questions aloud. The first question dealt with Porifera, which are sponges. The remaining questions were about bones, the liver, cells, spiders – the information was jumbled in regards to the order of the chapters, and the question did not follow the curriculum sequence. The student had enormous difficulty processing because he couldn't shift mental gears quickly enough. Simply grouping all the questions about invertebrates, for instance, or chunking all of the questions from Chapter 7, would have made a huge difference for him. It took the student four days to complete the 200-question Scantron test because of the added task of constantly shifting to new subject matter.

**Use white space to separate**

Students can become overwhelmed by seeing an enormous block of text on the page, so whenever possible, separate paragraphs with white space. This makes the content appear more "user-friendly."

# Mnemonics and Acrostics

Mnemonics, or memory devices, are terrific aids for students who have difficulty remembering key information. Mnemonics are effective because they give students a script or a checklist that can be followed as they complete an assignment or try to recall certain information. A common mnemonic that you may be familiar with is HOMES, which is the acronym for the names of the Great Lakes.

**Huron, Ontario, Michigan, Erie, Superior**

Another famous acronym helps music students recall the lines of the treble clef, EGBDF:

**Every Good Boy Deserves Favor**

An acrostic can be helpful for remembering a series of items, such as the planets, by taking the first letter of each word and creating a memorable sentence:

**Mercury Venus Earth Mars Jupiter Saturn Uranus Neptune**

**My Very Excellent Mother Just Served Us Nachos**

When my students were trying to remember the stages of mitosis (Interphase, Prophase, Metaphase, Anaphase, Telophase), they came up with the acrostic:

**I Party Mad And Tough.**

It is best for students to create their own memory devices so they "own" the memory. Another use of mnemonics and acrostics is to apply them in conjunction with another strategy to help students learn how to label diagrams and maps, which is difficult for students who have visual motor integration issues. These students suffer from an identified disability that prevents them from looking across a page and understanding the space. In order to help students memorize places on a map, I've given the idea of an acrostic a little twist.

On page 18, you'll see a map of South America. Starting with Venezuela at the top of the map, I drew a big letter S that bisected all of the countries that the students would be held accountable for knowing. Their assignment was to label the diagram. As a mnemonic device, they created a sentence from the acronym of the countries' names:

**Venezuela Columbia Ecuador Peru Brazil Paraguay Uruguay Argentina Chile Bolivia**

**Very Cold Elephants Put Big Pretty Underwear Around Children's Bottoms**

On a test, they had to label the countries on the map. In the past, students were given colored pencils to shade in the different countries. However, this did not organize the information into a sequence the students could recall from memory. Students who don't process well need a strategy to help them sequence the material. This technique provides them with the roadmap, and it's a lot of fun.

# Mapping Strategy for South America

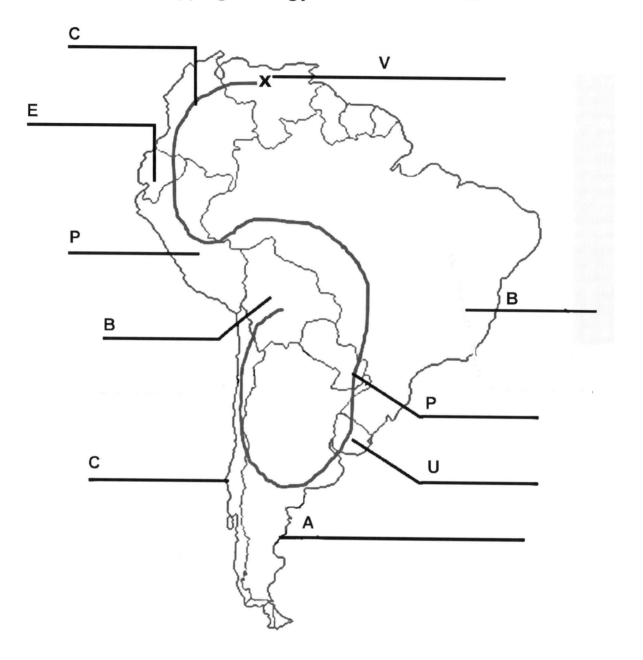

V _____  P _____

C _____  U _____

E _____  A _____

P _____  C _____

B _____  B _____

## Instructions for Mapping Strategy

Step 1: Put an "X" in the country shaped like a "V" to indicate a starting point.

Step 2: Draw the letter "S" to bisect the countries and create a roadmap.

Step 3: Create a mnemonic.

Step 4: Practice both the mnemonic and the associated country names.

Step 5: Practice labeling the countries.

### Practice Labeling Diagrams

Place diagrams in a plastic page protector. Students trace and label the diagram with a vis-a-vis marker on the plastic, which allows for multiple practice opportunities.

# Sequencing Events – The Curvy Line

Once in a while you'll see a notation on a modification page to "use visuals." The Curvy Line is a strategy that uses visuals to help students remember a sequence, an order or a process. It might be the process of division in math, or a story in language arts. In science, it might be the steps to a lab experiment; in social studies, the series of events that led to an important battle.

To use this strategy, a story is told in pictures. For the example on page 21, let's use chapter 133 of Herman Melville's novel, *Moby Dick*. The main events of that chapter are:

➤ At dawn, Ahab notices a smooth wake in the ocean, the sign of a large whale.

➤ The captain climbs the mainmast to watch for the whale. He is about two-thirds of the way to the top when he spies a water spout.

➤ The small whaleboats are lowered, but the whale disappears for an hour.

➤ A flock of white birds flies toward Ahab's boat, the sign that the whale is approaching.

➤ Ahab peers in the water and sees Moby Dick's white head coming up from the depths.

➤ Moby Dick opens his enormous jaws and bites the boat in two.

➤ Ahab is rescued, but the hunt is over for the day.

When you create visual notes on this chart, position key events at each curve. As the students' eyes travel back and forth across the page, the "visual shift" creates memory points in both sides of the brain. Memories that reside in multiple locations can still be accessed, even if one location is not available or has been compromised. By contrast, bulleted lists tend to lodge in one location. If a child has difficulty accessing that particular place in the brain, the entire memory may be lost.

You can teach your students to do this for themselves as a method of note taking. For the benefit of the whole class, you could ask a student with artistic skill to draw simple illustrations on the classroom board as you describe the process, series of events, or story. If you're using this technique in math, it might help to personify some of the concepts you're working with, which adds a bit of variety and ensures that the information sticks in the student's memory.

# The Curvy Line
## Chapter 133 of *Moby Dick* by Herman Melville

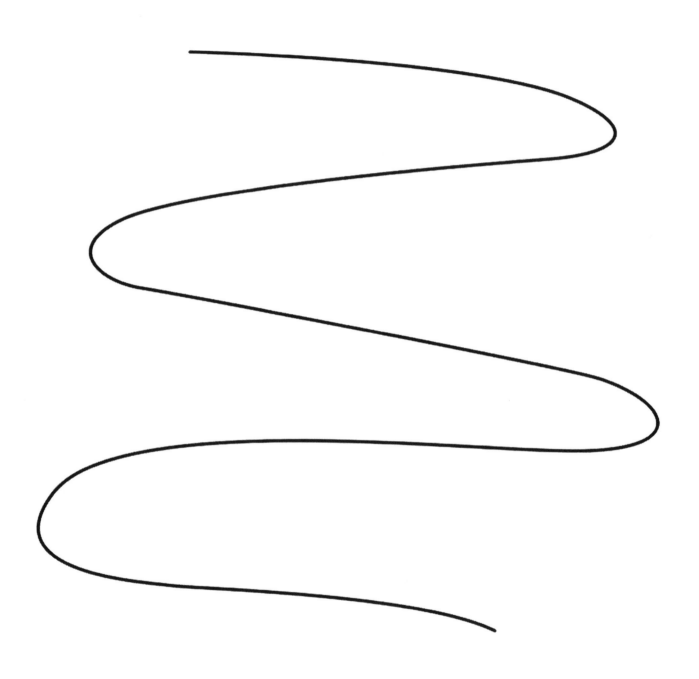

# Memory Chain Strategies

For students who have processing difficulties, it can often seem as if information falls into a black hole. A "linking strategy" is aimed at building a bridge across that black hole so that the processing of information can continue. Linking strategies are very effective in the secondary classroom.

## Creating memory chains

Many students with disabilities are visual learners, and they have trouble remembering the lessons in their textbooks. In order to help them create a memory chain, their teacher creates an illustration to explain a new concept. Advanced drawing skills are not a prerequisite for using this strategy. For instance, if the biology lesson focuses on brain cells, then as you explain the lesson, you would draw the axon, the dendrites, and indicate the spaces where the synapses occur.

This strategy works exceptionally well for students who experience difficulty learning. However, it's not appropriate for those who learn quickly.

## Flash cards with a twist

A standard vocabulary flashcard has the word on one side and the definition on the other. This version has a twist that helps students absorb the word's meaning. The basic rule of mnemonics is that you can remember any new piece of information as long as you attach it to something you already know.

Look at the example on page 24. I took a 3 x 5 index card and folded it in half, denoted by the dashed line. On the top half of the front, I placed the word in a balloon, which indicated that it was the real vocabulary word. On the top half of the back, I wrote the definition in another balloon.

This is where you begin building the bridge: give students some time to study the word and see if they come up with a connection on their own. If not, then you can help them brainstorm another word they already know. In this example, the vocabulary word the students needed to learn was "melancholy."

One of my students, Jen, could not connect the word "melancholy" with the definition "excessively gloomy." So the first step was to ask Jen, "What word do you already know that 'sounds like' or 'immediately reminds you' of the word melancholy." Jen responded, "It reminds me of the word jolly." So she wrote that on the bottom half of the front of the card – not in a balloon, the sign that it's the linking word. Flip the card over. On the side opposite the word "melancholy," the definition "excessively gloomy" is written in a balloon. On the bottom half of the back of the card, Jen writes a linking sentence (the sillier, the better) and draws a silly picture that links "excessively gloomy" to the word "jolly." She writes, "He went from being jolly to acting melancholy." In this case, she drew a happy face and an arrow pointing to a sad face. The research indicates that the picture is an essential part of the process and must not be skipped. When combined with the other four components (real word, linking word, linking sentence and real definition), the picture helps lock in the memory of the word. When this student studied her vocabulary cartoon cards, she would see her drawings of the happy and sad faces and think, "He went from being jolly to being really sad. Oh, right! Excessively gloomy means really sad."

That's how you build the bridge for those students who have problems with processing and linking.

## Vocabulary Cartoons
### Creating Visual Memory Chains

1.  Vocabulary word
2.  Definition
3.  Linking Word

4.  Linking sentence
5.  Linking picture

# Vocabulary Cartoons, Version II

This technique uses a sheet of paper, which can be three-hole punched and placed in the vocabulary section of students' binders. This makes a terrific study guide and may be preferable to 3 x 5 cards, which often wind up scattered and lost.

Create five columns and five rows, filled in as follows:

| Real word | Linking word | Linking sentence | Linking picture | Real definition |
|---|---|---|---|---|

Here's an example in this format:

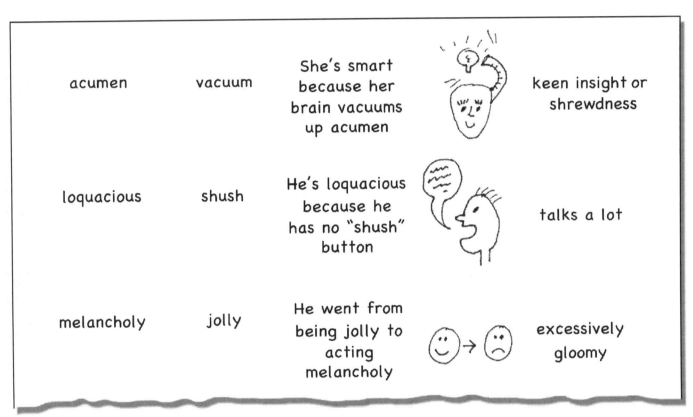

| acumen | vacuum | She's smart because her brain vacuums up acumen | | keen insight or shrewdness |
| loquacious | shush | He's loquacious because he has no "shush" button | | talks a lot |
| melancholy | jolly | He went from being jolly to acting melancholy | | excessively gloomy |

Once you have filled in your columns and rows, fold the paper in half, then fold it in half again. The middle column will be bisected by the paper fold, but that's okay. Now fold back the first and last columns, as though you were folding back the flaps on a paper airplane. For study purposes, those two flaps can be held next to each other. The student looks down the list of vocabulary words, checking his ability to remember the real definitions against the answers on the last flap. If additional help is needed, the paper can be opened up, displaying the linking word, sentence and picture.

| acumen | keen insight or shrewdness |
| loquacious | talks a lot |
| melancholy | excessively gloomy |

# Memory Chain worksheet

| Real Word | Reminding Word | Reminding Sentence | Reminding Picture | Real Definition |
|-----------|----------------|--------------------|--------------------|-----------------|
|           |                |                    |                    |                 |
|           |                |                    |                    |                 |
|           |                |                    |                    |                 |
|           |                |                    |                    |                 |
|           |                |                    |                    |                 |

# TEACHING TIP

## The Power of Repetition

How many times does a student need to be exposed to a new piece of information before it is committed to memory? According to research led by C.H. Hargis, a high ability student with an IQ of 120 needs approximately 25 repetitions in order to acquire new information. Many students with learning disabilities have an IQ of about 100, and they need about 35 repetitions. Students on the low end of the IQ spectrum and at-risk learners may need up to 55 repetitions to learn something new. Many students don't understand just how many repetitions are needed to memorize new material.

In light of this research, one science teacher placed a review bar with a series of check boxes on his worksheets (see page 110). When a sponge activity was needed, the teacher would ask students to pull out their notes on a particular topic—in this case, cell reproduction. He would have them pair up, summarize their notes to each other and quiz each other on the notes. Each time the students completed this activity, they would put a check in one of the boxes. After they had done this six times, they would be on their way to the number of repetitions needed to commit the information to memory. The exercise showed students that there is a difference between homework and study, and it pointed out that study required many repetitions.

# Behavior Reminders (RESPECT)

I surveyed middle school teachers in a Connecticut city and asked them to define the greatest behavioral challenge that they faced with their students. They unanimously said it was disrespectful behavior. What I was surprised to find was that every teacher defined respect differently. Students were receiving mixed messages because what one teacher would not tolerate because it was viewed as disrespectful, another teacher didn't mind in her classroom (for example, gum chewing).

In a 6th grade language arts class in one city school, students were learning how to create acrostics. We devised a poster contest: who could come up with the best acrostic for the word "Respect"? To help them brainstorm this activity, we provided the following T-chart:

RESPECT

| What does respectful behavior look like? | What does respectful behavior sound like? |
|---|---|
| | |

Students brainstormed both the visual and the auditory aspects of respect, then used that information to create their posters. All around the school, we displayed the Respect acrostic posters, and we invited some dignitaries to judge the contest. The text from the winning poster is on page 24. All of the teachers agreed to use this poster as the basis for behavioral standards in the classroom, to determine which behaviors would be reinforced, and which would be punished.

Here's how it was implemented in the classroom: if a student answered a question in a nice tone of voice (for a change), the teacher might say, "Good answer, and I like the way you spoke in a nice tone of voice. You're being very respectful." On the other hand, if a student was slouching in his or her chair, the teacher might say, "You need to sit up. You're being disrespectful because you're not exhibiting good body language."

It became really clear to students what behaviors were expected. When all the teachers agreed to reinforce the same standards of respectful behavior, a shift in culture occurred. Students were much more respectful in classrooms and common areas of the school, as evidenced by the reduced number of office referrals for disrespectful behaviors.

**R**esponds using appropriate words

**E**xpresses ideas at appropriate times

**S**peaks in a nice tone of voice

**P**olitely uses a clear indoor volume

**E**xhibits good body language

**C**omplies with teacher requests

**T**imely compliance (within 2 minutes)

# SPECIAL STRATEGY

## Question-directed strategy

Sometimes we have students that ask questions because they want to lead their teacher off task. These students seem to know that if they can take us somewhere else, we will lose the momentum of the lesson. In that case, put up five fingers, which means you'll take only five questions. As the students ask questions, put a finger down. It helps move the lesson along when you show students you want five ideas. They understand that's the limit, and it's also a good visual reminder.

In the event you have one student that monopolizes the question-directed routine, give that student two 3 x 5 cards. Tell the student that he will be limited to two questions over the next 20 minutes and he should ask them wisely. Each time that student asks a question (no matter how mundane, i.e., "Can I sharpen my pencil?" or complex, "Can you restate the directions?"), you remove a 3 x 5 card. This acts as a visual reminder for the student and limits verbal output.

# DIFFERENTIATED STRATEGIES

# Visualization

Many students with disabilities have difficulty creating a visual image of the subject matter they study. As a result, it is hard for them to recall information. This technique will expand their ability to visualize, resulting in improved content retention. When we teach students how to create their own visuals, they develop into independent learners.

Occasionally I need to pre-teach visualization by teaching a student how to "storyboard." (Please see "Sketch Notes" on pages 115-117.) Once students have mastered how to visually capture a series of events, then we can teach them how to use visualizations to increase their ability to remember important material.

Explain to students that you are going to teach them how to make "movies" in their heads, and then have them follow these steps for visualization:

- ➤ Create a mental image by "painting a backdrop." (If you're reading about trees, imagine a forest. If the subject matter is someone eating, picture yourself at a diner holding a sandwich and taking a bite.)

- ➤ Manipulate the image to make it memorable:

    1. Make the image big
    2. Make the image weird
    3. Make the image move
    4. Add details

- ➤ Create a chain of pictures: invent one scene that leads to another.

Always remember to first teach the strategy using easy material, and apply it to coursework only after the students have mastered the technique. One way to teach the visualization strategy before applying it to a particular lesson is to tell a silly story.

The Visualization Lesson on pages 35-37 was one of my favorite strategies to use in my 10th grade study skills class, and my students loved it too. There may be times when pre-teaching the concept of common nouns will be required before moving to the first step.

# Visualization Lesson
## Tell a Silly Story

Objective: Teach students to create mental pictures in order to help them remember a sequence of events.

Lesson:

1. Working as a group, have students list ten common nouns.

2. Facilitate while students create memorable nouns, using the visualization rules. (Make the image big and weird, make it move, and add details.) Link the nouns together by creating a narrative that runs from one noun to the next.

3. Once the story is finished, erase or cover up the nouns. Have students try to write down all ten nouns in the original order.

4. Add another level of challenge to the activity by asking the students to write the nouns in reverse order. By writing the last noun first and moving backwards to the first noun, the story is reversed and the facts are committed more solidly to memory.

| Nouns | The story |
|-------|-----------|
| 1. | |
| 2. | |
| 3. | |
| 4. | |
| 5. | |
| 6. | |
| 7. | |
| 8. | |
| 9. | |
| 10. | |

Step 1: List ten common nouns on the classroom board, as in this example:

1.  Dog
2.  Cat
3.  Fish
4.  Car
5.  House
6.  Tree
7.  Arms
8.  Apple
9.  School
10. Key

Step 2: Transform the ten common nouns so that they become memorable by using the four rules of visualization. Here is an example from my classroom:

1.  The dog is not just any dog. He's a big, huge, red dog. Imagine him sitting in a yard and along comes...

2.  ...a cat, but not just any cat. This cat is weird because she has purple fur with yellow stripes. She climbs on the red dog's back to take a nap. All of a sudden, out of the sky falls a...

3.  ...fish. Not just a normal fish, but a two-headed fish with five eyeballs: two on each side and one in the middle for good measure. The two-headed fish falls smack on the big red dog's head. The dog is shocked and shakes his head, which propels the fish through the air. The fish lands in my...

4.  ...car: my gold-plated sports car. The fish landing on my car startles me, so I drive off the road and I drive into a...

5.  ...house. It happens to be a movie star's house (students always had fun determining which movie star it should be). The movie star comes out of the house and says, "Are you okay? Why don't you get out of the car to collect yourself and come sit down under this..."

6.  ...tree. It's a bizarre tree because instead of branches, it has...

7.  ...arms. I'm looking up thinking, "This tree is bizarre, it has arms." And in one of the hands on the tree's arm is one huge...

8   ...apple with pink and blue polka dots. Gravity takes over and the polka dot apple falls out of the tree and cracks open right at my feet. Inside the apple, instead of a core, is a...

9   ...school. As I look at this mini-school, I wonder how the teachers entered the tiny door. Along comes the purple cat with the yellow stripes. In his mouth he has a...

10  ...key. The purple cat with the yellow stripes unlocks the school door, but when he's done, the key sprouts legs and runs away.

Step 3: Once you reach the end of the story, erase the list of nouns. Then have students write the list of nouns from memory. If the nouns were remarkable, the success rate should be pretty high.

If the students forget one or two words, it's likely that the words occurred in the middle of the story. That's because the content in the middle is always harder to remember. To help students with this issue, encourage them to embellish and add more details to that area of the story to make it come alive.

Step 4: Ask the students to cover up the list of nouns with a new sheet of paper, then have them write the nouns in reverse order from memory.

Students might use any one of several strategies to recall the reverse order. Some will mentally play the story to the end, remember the last two nouns, write those down, play the story down again, get the two nouns before that, write those down, and so on. That's essentially a chunking strategy.

Students with disabilities have a hard time working backward. This becomes apparent when you ask them to think back to an earlier chapter. For instance, if you are currently teaching Chapter 7 and you try to relate the information back to what was discussed in Chapter 3, students with disabilities often have a difficult time making that leap.

One linking strategy that can help students make this leap is retracing the steps that led to the current lesson. As an example, you might want everyone to remember what was discussed in Chapter 3. To help students make those links, we sometimes must start at the beginning and move forward to the present, rather than asking them to look back. "We talked about topic A, which led to topic B in Chapter 4, topic C in Chapter 5, topic D in Chapter 6, and that's how it all relates to topic E in Chapter 7."

It's easy to see how to use the visualization strategy in language arts, doing what we just did – sequencing a story and adding bizarre details.

In history, you might sequence the events of a battle. In that case, you would list ten to twelve keywords, and then go down the list and tell the story of the battle in detail. Next, have students practice writing the list down so that they remember the sequence of events that led to an important point.

In mathematics you might employ visualization to teach the steps for dividing numbers. To make the lesson memorable, it helps to personify symbols. For instance, have the students visualize a cat dragging a division sign across the room, or a multiplication sign that runs around on spindly legs. Especially when you need to liven up the middle of the period, this exercise may provide a fun interlude.

# Associative Techniques

We naturally use associative techniques when we retrace our steps to find a lost checkbook or car keys. One such associative technique is called "internal scripting." We simply retrace our steps by talking to ourselves: "I came in and put my coat down. Then the phone rang and I answered it..."

Many students with disabilities have difficulty remembering an order or a sequence. To support the internal scripting process, teach them to create checklists. Associating a mnemonic with these lists is doubly helpful. For example, if some students have difficulty getting started with a task, you might use the word 'WORK' to create a mnenomic that stands for: **W**rite your name on the page, **O**rganize your thoughts, **R**ead the directions and **K**eep your attention on the first item.

Another technique that can help students create an internal script is the "think out loud" method. To illustrate this technique, imagine a math teacher who wants to demonstrate how to add decimals. One usual way of teaching this might be to describe the steps using the YOU point of view. "You line up the decimal point..." An effective alternative is to describe the steps from the "I" point of view, which cues your students to do it the same way. It may not seem like much of a strategy, but it can make a big difference. By using the word "I," you give your students an internal script.

"I'm going to demonstrate how I would do this example. I'm going to talk it through out loud to show you how I am thinking inside my head. And then when it's your turn to practice these examples on the worksheet, what I want you to do is talk it through with a partner in the same manner that I'm demonstrating it to you." Students then practice thinking out loud with a partner, each taking a turn talking through the process. In addition to helping students create an internal script, it also uses a peer tutoring technique to reteach the material. Each student hears the information three times: once from the teacher, once from their partner, and once from themselves.

When a student is given the assignment to add 17.3 + 5.2, his thought process might go as follows: "My teacher says I must remember to line up my decimals, so I did that. So I know the first thing I do is I start from the right hand side. 3 plus 2 is 5 tenths. I put that down, go over here. 7 plus 5 is – oh, what is it? 12. I put down the 2 and I carry the 1, which is a "10" at the top of the tens column. Now I have 10 plus 10 and that's 20, and I represent the 20 with a 2 in the tens column." *

Students with disabilities are frequently self-conscious about being 'different,' of doing something that is not appropriate. I teach my students that talking through the steps in their heads can be a very productive learning technique. When they hear that it's what good learners and students in college do, that helps to remove any uncertainty.

*Under the common core, it is very important to represent the appropriate place value with our math models.

# Color Coding

In some of their research, Sydney Zentall and her colleagues discovered that certain colors contribute to enhanced memory. Her research showed the top memory color as red, but since red doesn't work well as a highlighter, a handy alternative is pink. Try offering students a pink highlighter rather than a yellow one. You may be surprised how certain colors enhance memory.

When you hand students highlighters, they may behave as if they were back in elementary school and it's coloring time. They may not yet be familiar with what should be highlighted, and may use the pens indiscriminately. That's where erasable highlighters can be very useful. One end of the pen applies the highlighting, and the eraser at the other end removes the color.

Color coding is a data collection technique as well as a teaching technique.

Let's assume you need your students to work with a piece of text. You ask them to work on their own to identify the main ideas by highlighting them in yellow. Collect the yellow highlighters and pass out blue ones. Now direct students to the items that they should have identified, and ask them to highlight those areas in blue. When a blue highlighter is used over a yellow one, it creates a patch of green. So, let's examine what the three highlighting colors indicate after the completion of this exercise. If the paper is covered in yellow highlighter, that's an indication that the student needs more instruction in note taking and identifying key elements. Too much blue means the student did not understand the concept of Main Idea and needs more instruction in identifying the main idea. If the paper if mostly green, then the student has mastered the skill and is ready for some enrichment, or to move on to the next skill.

Other items that can be used in color coding:

➢ Highlight tape (available at local office supply stores).

➢ Assorted novelty highlighters (available regionally) that are erasable, "magic" or disappearing, or scented.

➢ Color coded sticky flags or notes, to be used in a textbook (example: use yellow for vocabulary, red for key ideas, etc.)

➢ A highlight window, created from colored clear food wrap. (Use an Exacto knife to cut a "window" out of a 3 x 5 card. Cover the window with a colored plastic wrap and secure with clear tape. The student uses the window to help them focus on reading by moving the window over the reading materials.

➢ A clear yellow or clear blue clipboard, clipped to a worksheet so that it shows through the back of the clipboard. The student uses a wet erase pen to write on the clipboard (but not the worksheet), which provides multiple practice opportunities on one worksheet.

➢ The use of multiple colors and highlighting on your technology board, tablet, or white board to help students focus on key parts of the curriculum.

# The Fishbowl

Social learning behaviors are essential skills to develop for common core access. The Fishbowl is a cooperative-learning structure for a small-group discussion or a partner discussion, which teaches students interaction skills. It also provides students with instruction in key learning behaviors, such as being able to "defend" or "justify" their answers. This method needs to be explicitly taught as part of the constructs of the classroom.

Here is how you create the Fishbowl method:

1. Create a rubric for your fishbowl for both participants and observers.

2. Teach each role through role modeling and role play.

3. Provide students with a well-defined discussion point. Give students private thinking time to construct and practice what they will say in the fish bowl activity.

4. Observe students, observe a group or pair of students engaging in a discussion about their ideas.

5. Observers sit in pre-determined locations near the activity (it is often best to have students stand around the activity in close proximity) and take notes on the fishbowl activity (notes on: strength of conversation (concise, makes sense, uses evidence..), quality of listening skills (verbal AND non-verbal), value of results (points made, lessons learned, conclusions..). Observers are graded on their fishbowl note-taking.

6. Fishbowl students are graded by the teacher on the same three skills above (see pages 41-42). Time the fishbowl activity and be sure everyone has equal time to speak and listen.

7. Observers share their findings and give feedback. (Compliment, pros of activity, lessons learned from Fishbowl team, suggestions for improvement)

Possible mistakes:

1. Allowing observers to be at desks away from the conversation (proximity is key.)

2. Allowing observers to make no feedback suggestions for improvement.

3. Allowing too much time for the activity (start with five to seven minutes).

Things to remember:

1. Pre-set students by organizing materials and practicing the needed language with fishbowl groups

2. Practice behaviors and key observation points with observers

3. Provide feedback to observers on the quality and depth of their observation.

4. Provide feedback to the Fishbowl team on suggestions for rubric improvement.

## Collaboration FISHBOWL Rubric

adapted from *University of Wisconsin-Stout (www.uwstout.edu) Collaboration Rubric*

| CATEGORY | Exemplary | Proficient | Partially Proficient | Unsatisfactory |
|---|---|---|---|---|
| | 3 points | 2 points | 1 point | 0 points |
| Task Participation and Problem Solving | Consistently stays focused on the task and what needs to be done. Very self-directed. Encouraging. Actively looks for and suggests solutions to problems. | Focuses on the task and what needs to be done most of the time. Other group members can count on this person. Makes one or two positive comments. Refines solutions suggested by others. | Focuses on the task and what needs to be done some of the time. Other group members must sometimes remind this person to keep on task. Does not suggest or refine solutions, but is willing to try out solutions suggested by others | Rarely focuses on the task and what needs to be done. Lets others do the work. Negative comments made. Does not try to solve problems or help others solve problems. |
| | 3 points | 2 points | 1 point | 0 points |
| Listening, Questioning and Discussing | Respectfully listens, interacts, discusses and poses questions to all members of the team during discussions and helps direct the group in reaching consensus. | Respectfully listens, interacts, discusses and poses questions to others during discussions. | Has some difficulty respectfully listening and discussing and/or tends to dominate discussions. | Has great difficulty listening, argues with teammates, and is unwilling to consider other opinions. Impedes group from reaching consensus. |
| TOTAL POINTS | ____ /6 | | | |

# COOPERATIVE LEARNING FOR FISHBOWL RUBRIC

*adapted from: www.sanmarinohs.org*

Title of Assignment :_____

*ALL STUDENTS WILL BE ABLE TO*:

Accept and complete assigned role and/or mutually agreed upon tasks.
Listen and respond constructively to others' ideas and criticism.
Build, reach, and support consensus when the task requires a group decision or conclusion.

RUBRIC (5 POINTS)

5   Student demonstrates exemplary cooperation through participation in the definition, organization, and completion of tasks through:

> ➤ listening respectfully and actively to others in the group

> ➤ participating equally and appropriately in the final group presentation, whether it be written or oral

> ➤ demonstrating respect for others in the group

> ➤ accepting constructive criticism

> ➤ working for the good of the group rather than for personal recognition by building and supporting consensus

4   Student demonstrates adequate cooperation through participation in the definition, organization, and completion of tasks through:

> ➤ listening respectfully to others

> ➤ completing assigned tasks

> ➤ participating in any final group presentation

3   Student participates to some degree on assigned tasks, group discussions, and the final group presentation, but does not consistently demonstrate the behaviors listed in point 4.

2   Student participates infrequently in group discussion and participates minimally in task completion.

1   Student does not participate in group discussion, nor attend to task completion.

# Graphic Organizers

*"You must never tell a thing. You must illustrate it.*
*We learn through the eye and not the noggin." – Will Rogers*

Graphic organizers are visual tools that can be used to enhance students' ability to recall information. A few important points to bear in mind when using them:

- Select the graphic organizer that is appropriate for the content being taught. Here are three types we typically use in the classroom:

  - Maps

  - Task organizers

  - Thinking and processing maps

- When a graphic organizer contains lines that connect one shape to another, University of Kansas Center for Research on Learning researchers have found that it's helpful to write a transition word or phrase on those lines, such as: "leads to" "because" or "is the result of."

- Give students detailed instructions about how to use the organizer.

- Practice using the organizer with your students. Do not assume that students with a disabilities automatically know how to use or fill in a graphic organizer.

## Maps

It's difficult for students with visual processing issues to decipher brainstorming spider maps, where satellite circles branch off from a circle in the center. Avoid confusion by using boxes rather than circles. The reproducibles on pages 44 and 45 are graphic organizers that you might find useful.

There are four main types of map organizers:

- Webs (box and line)
  - A box web is based on the circle web that is frequently used by teachers. The boxes make it a bit more "user friendly" for students with disabilities.
  - Line webs can be confusing for some students.
- Mind maps
- Story maps
- Cluster Maps vs. Concept Trees

Reproducible
# Box Web

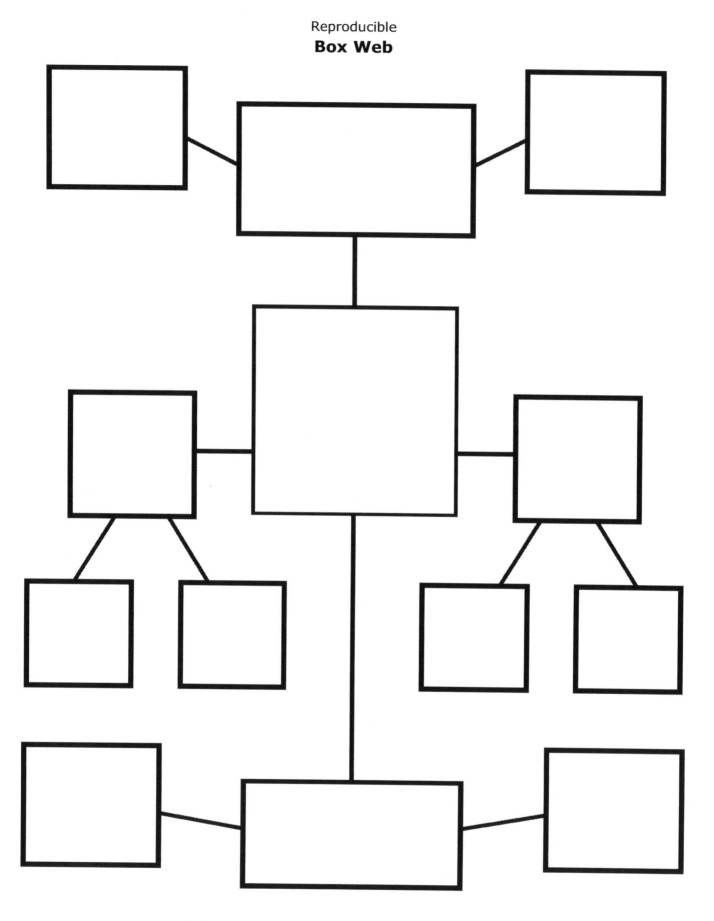

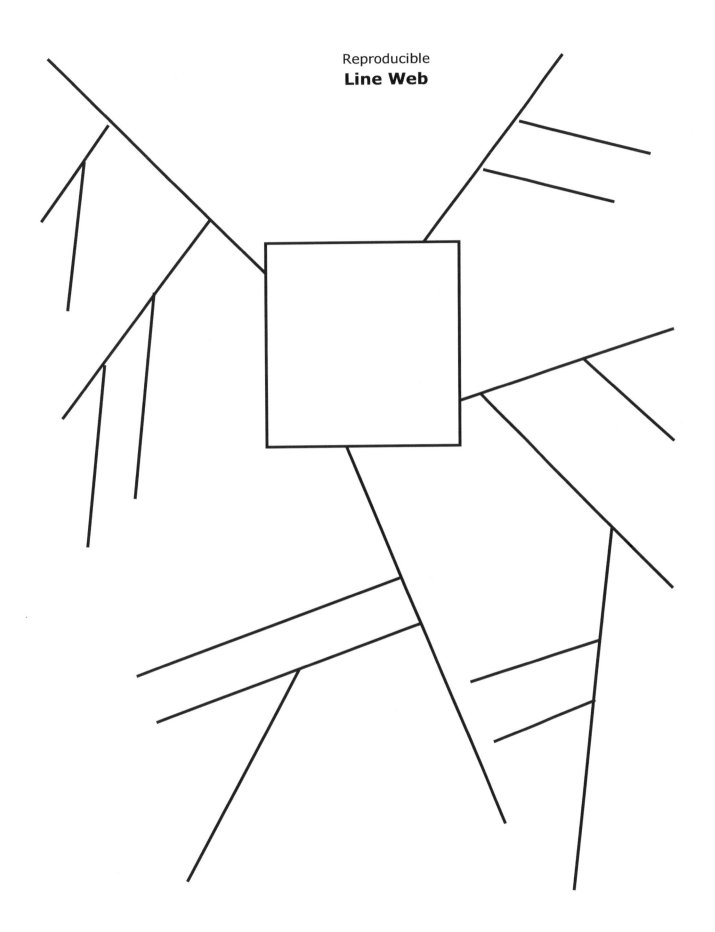

# How to Grow a Concept Tree

A concept tree features boxes that fan out from a base via "branches." It can be oriented in any direction. This kind of organizer provides students with a concrete sequential approach to a seemingly random task. Here are basic instructions for building a concept tree:

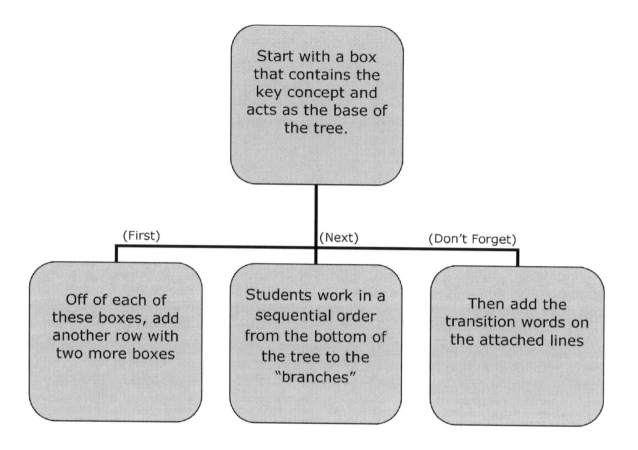

TEACHING TIP

**Preheat the writing process**

Have students brainstorm ideas on sticky notes and arrange the information in a sensible order. Then have them transfer the sticky notes onto a concept tree, which is another example of a tactile graphic organizer. An accommodation could consist of having students use the concept tree instead of an outline.

© Sonya Heineman Kunkel, 2013  P a g e  46

# Concept Tree

*Add a transition word to each arrow

# Task Organizers

To help ensure that your students stay focused on a specific aspect of an assignment, try any of these task organizers:

<u>Compare and Contrast</u> (page 50) When using compare and contrast charts, you might try having students work in the columns instead of the rows. For example, have them list all of the points of comparison or the points of contrasts. Then list all of the perspectives for one point, then the perspectives for the second point. Finally summarize <u>how</u> the points are the "same." For example, have them first list all the points regarding how the North and the South were the same during the Civil War. Then list why the North was the same (Point A), and then how the South was the same. Finally, add a summary statement about this point. By the time the students are done, they have the skeleton of a paragraph for a compare/contrast writing assignment.

<u>Cause and Effect</u> (page 51) This organizer works well for a science class or a history class where there may be multiple problems to solve. Depending upon which problem you choose, there is potentially more than one solution, which in turn leads to various effects. Students learn that problem solving is not necessarily linear. Ideally, this translates into an understanding of the big picture: that there's not always a perfect problem with a perfect solution that has a perfect effect. Problem solving is a very fluid process. Variations could be problem-solution and cause-effect.

<u>Chapter Outliner</u> (page 52) Creating outlines helps students clarify their thoughts, which facilitates the writing process. This task organizer helps students take notes on a reading assignment by guiding them through the process of outlining. This organizer should be available to all students, regardless of learning ability. Some students are skilled at taking notes and outlining with a freeform method; however, even advanced students may find this chart helpful.

<u>Paragraph Summary</u> (page 53) This organizer helps students who have difficulty reading. When they break a chapter down into paragraphs, it improves their reading comprehension and note taking skills. Students assign a "heading" or title to each paragraph. Next to each star, they list the important keywords that were encountered. For the summary, students write a one-sentence paraphrase of the paragraph. By reformulating concepts in their own words, students process the information rather than merely parroting it. Information retention is improved.

<u>3-D Organizers</u> such as a Venn Diagram made out of hula hoops with sticky notes (see page 126). Students with disabilities perform better when they can kinesthetically participate in their work. This is due in part to the fact that many students with disabilities have strongly developed kinesthetic learning styles.

<u>Other ways to create 3D organizers</u>

- Students apply 3 x 5 cards to large chart paper on a wall.

- Use an interactive device, such as an electronic board or electronic tablet.

- Have students use manipulatives to show items on a graph.

- Use a checkerboard and checkers to demonstrate the concept of slope.

The possibilities are endless.

# Compare and Contrast

| Point of Comparison | A | B | How they are alike |
|---|---|---|---|
|  |  |  |  |
|  |  |  |  |
|  |  |  |  |
|  |  |  |  |

| Point of Contrast | A | B | How they are different |
|---|---|---|---|
|  |  |  |  |
|  |  |  |  |
|  |  |  |  |
|  |  |  |  |

**Cause and Effect**

We often find that one cause has several effects...

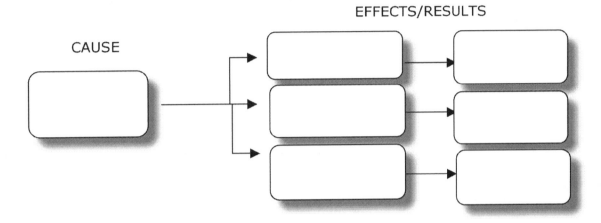

EFFECTS/RESULTS

CAUSE

...and that several causes lead to one effect.

CAUSE

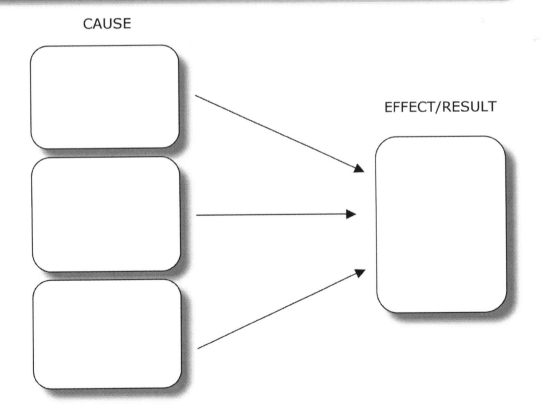

EFFECT/RESULT

# Chapter Outliner

Name _____

Date Due _____

Title of this Unit _____

Title of this Chapter _____

Points to Understand

- _____
- _____
- _____
- _____
- _____
- _____
- _____
- _____
- _____

Vocabulary and Definitions

1. _____
2. _____
3. _____
4. _____
5. _____
6. _____
7. _____
8. _____
9. _____
10. _____

# Paragraph Summary

Chapter title: _____

| Heading _____ | Heading _____ |
|---|---|
| * _____ | * _____ |
| * _____ | * _____ |
| * _____ | * _____ |
| * _____ | * _____ |
| * _____ | * _____ |
| Summary _____ | Summary _____ |
| _____ | _____ |
| Heading _____ | Heading _____ |
| * _____ | * _____ |
| * _____ | * _____ |
| * _____ | * _____ |
| * _____ | * _____ |
| * _____ | * _____ |
| Summary _____ | Summary _____ |
| _____ | _____ |
| Heading _____ | Heading _____ |
| * _____ | * _____ |
| * _____ | * _____ |
| * _____ | * _____ |
| * _____ | * _____ |
| * _____ | * _____ |
| * _____ | * _____ |
| Summary _____ | Summary _____ |
| _____ | _____ |
| Heading _____ | Heading _____ |
| * _____ | * _____ |
| * _____ | * _____ |
| * _____ | * _____ |
| * _____ | * _____ |
| * _____ | * _____ |
| * _____ | |
| Summary _____ | Summary _____ |
| _____ | _____ |

**Thinking Process Maps**

All students can benefit from a little help structuring and organizing their thoughts, but students with disabilities need extra assistance when introduced to a new concept. Thinking process maps help students discover connections between ideas, sort out what they know, and chart their progress.

➤ Concept sorter (Anchoring Table)

➤ KWL (Know-Want-Learned Chart)

➤ Predictions

➤ Processing and connections (Lesson Closer)

**Anchoring Table**

When introduced to a new concept, students often have a difficult time storing the idea in the appropriate mental file box. Use the reproducible on page 55 to help students organize their thoughts.

Example 1

Concept/topic: Polygons

Essential characteristics: It's a figure that has at least three sides and it is closed.

Non-essential characteristics: the number of sides can equal more than three.

Examples: triangle, square, dodecahedron.

Non-examples: line, circle

In this way, as students learn a concept, they learn what it *must* have, what it *might* look like, and what it definitely could *not* be. That helps the students anchor the concept in a number of ways.

Example 2

Concept/topic: Vertebrates

Essential characteristics: an animal with a backbone.

Non essential characteristics: warm or cold-blooded, has scales or fur

Examples: fish, human, dog

Non-examples: protozoa, sea cucumber, jellyfish

# Anchoring Table

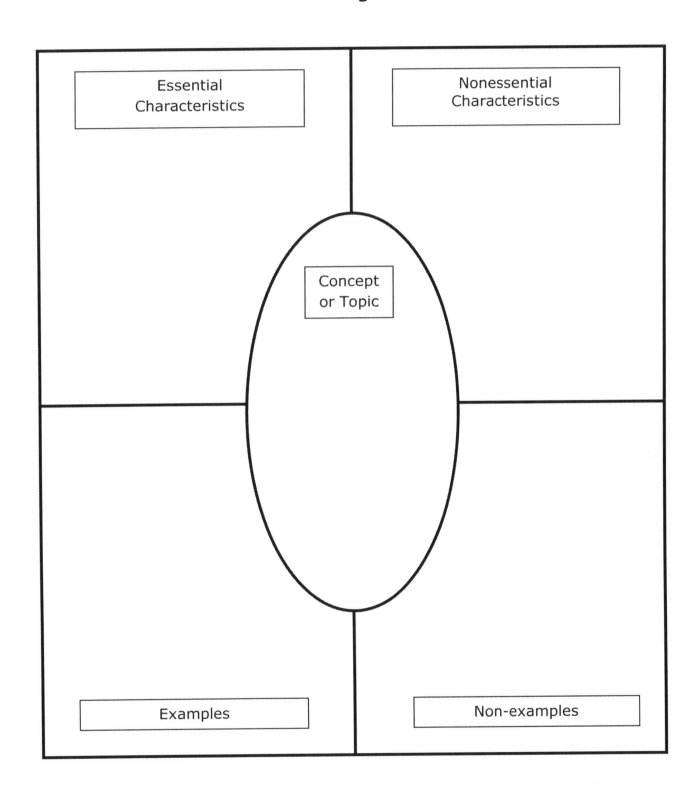

Essential
Characteristics

Nonessential
Characteristics

Concept
or Topic

Examples

Non-examples

## K-W-L Table

On page 57, there is a K-W-L table that you may find useful. At the beginning of a unit, I ask my students, "What do you know about this topic?" At the end of a week I ask them, "What would you like to know?" And at the end of the unit, the question is, "Tell me what you've learned."

Learning can be broken down into three parts:

1. What strategies did you learn?
2. What cooperative group techniques did you learn?
3. What material did you learn in the content?

Students are often surprised at how much they have learned about a particular topic. It anchors them and helps them focus on acquiring knowledge for its own sake, rather than learning only as a means of passing a test.

Most parents are familiar with the frustration that occurs from this exchange:

Parent: "What'd you learn in school today?"

Child: "Nothing."

Filling out this chart gives students a clear idea of what they have learned, so perhaps they'll be able to answer that eternal question a bit more to their parents' satisfaction.

## Lesson Closer

Another thing that might help students anchor new information is the Lesson Closer on page 58. If you have some spare time after the lesson, this can be a fun way to encourage reflection on what they've just learned by either writing down or drawing some of the concepts.

➢ Three important points from today

➢ Ideas that are square (or good) with me

➢ Topics that I still need to think about

➢ Ideas that are still going around in my head

# The K-W-L Table

| What I **K**now | What I **W**ant to Know | What I **L**earned |
| --- | --- | --- |
| | | |

# Lesson Closer

Three important points from today:

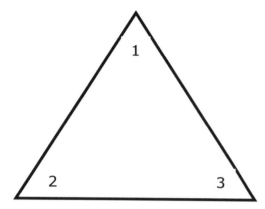

Ideas that are square with me:

Things I still need to think about:

Going around in my head is:

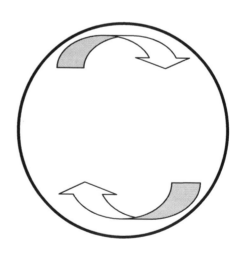

## Inspiration

Inspiration.com sells applications that generate prefab graphic organizers, or assist you in creating your own. The program includes color-coding options and a wide variety of pictures to choose from. One helpful feature of this program is its ability to transform a graphic organizer into an outline with the push of a button. This has proven beneficial to students who stall in the writing process because they have difficulty turning a brainstorming session into an outline.

www.inspiration.com

For those working with non-verbal students, Inspiration provides another bit of assistive technology called Kidspiration. These graphic organizers are more picture-oriented to help visual learners. They can be accessed through the Inspiration website, or directly via:

www.kidspiration.com

Here's another site that has free graphic organizer templates:

http://creately.com/Free-K12-Education-Templates

Demonstrating how students can create their own customized graphic organizers helps them become independent learners, which should always be a teacher's goal. The goal of special education should be to teach a student independence. Consider teaching students how to make their own graphic organizers as a goal instead of giving them a graphic organizer to fill in. The first is an example of Specially Designed Instruction aimed at creating independence through self-sustaining methods, the second an accommodation that supports the student with and external locus of control, whereby the student is a passive learner.

Don't forget to check your "app store." There are many creative applications available for smart phones, smart tablets, electronic classroom boards, and personal computers.

# Who I Am Makes A Difference

Teaching isn't always easy, and teachers often feel unappreciated. Before we move on to the next section, I'd like to share a story by an unknown author, which I find inspiring.

A teacher in New York decided to honor each of her seniors in high school by telling them they made a difference to her. So she called each student, one at a time, to the front of the class. First she told them how they had made a difference to her in her class. Then she presented each one of them with a blue ribbon emblazoned with the words, "Who I Am Makes A Difference."

Afterwards, the teacher initiated a class project to measure the impact of recognition on a community. She gave each student three blue ribbons and asked them to go forth and spread the recognition ceremony. One student approached a junior executive who had helped him with his career planning process. He said:

"You really made a difference in my career planning. I'd like to give you this ribbon."

The young executive was pleasantly surprised and responded, "Why, thank you!"

The student continued: "We're doing a class project, and I was wondering if I could give you these two other ribbons and have you keep the recognition ceremony going. Would you please get back to me about this recognition ceremony so I can tell my class?"

The junior executive agreed and took the two blue ribbons. Later that day he went to see his boss, who was known as being kind of a grouchy fellow. The junior executive sat his boss down and told him that he admired him for being a creative genius. The boss seemed very surprised. The junior executive asked him if he would accept the gift of a blue ribbon and give him permission to affix it to his jacket. The surprised boss said, "Well... sure."

Then the junior executive handed his boss the third blue ribbon and said, "I'm doing this for a kid in high school, and I wonder if you could take this last blue ribbon and continue this acknowledgement ceremony, and then get back to me and let me know what happened." The boss agreed and accepted the last blue ribbon.

That night the boss went home to his 14-year-old son. He sat him down and said, "The most incredible thing happened to me today. I was in my office and one of the junior executives came in and told me he admired me, and he gave me a blue ribbon for being a creative genius. Imagine, he thinks *I'm* a creative genius. And he put this blue ribbon on me that says 'Who I Am Makes a Difference.' He gave me an extra blue ribbon and asked me to find somebody to honor. So as I was driving home today, I started to think about who I would honor, and I thought I would honor you. My days are hectic, sometimes I yell at you for not doing your homework or not cleaning your room, but you make a difference to me. Along with your mother, you're the most important person in my life and I love you." The startled boy burst into tears. He couldn't compose himself. His entire body shook. He looked up at his father and said through his tears:

"Dad, earlier tonight I sat in my room and wrote a letter to you and mom explaining to you why I had killed myself and asking you to forgive me. I was going to commit suicide tonight after you were asleep. I just didn't think you all cared. The letter is upstairs. I don't think I'll need it after all."

His father walked upstairs and found the heartfelt letter full of anguish and pain. The envelope was addressed to Mom and Dad.

The boss went back to work a changed man. He was no longer a grouch. Instead, he made sure to let his employees know that they had made a difference to him.

The junior executive helped several other young people in their career planning and never forgot to let them know that they had made a difference in *his* life.

And the young boy and his classmates learned a valuable lesson.

Who you are *does* make a difference. Please accept this virtual blue ribbon, because I know that if you try these strategies in your classroom, that you'll make a difference in somebody's life.

# MODIFYING and UNDERSTANDING the IEP

# Introduction to Modifications

During my seminars around the country, I am asked certain questions time and again:

> ➤ Why must we modify for students with disabilities?

> ➤ Am I required to modify for students with disabilities?

> ➤ Don't we run the risk of enabling some of these kids?

> ➤ Are some of these kids simply lazy?

The answers to those questions will become apparent as we work through this section.

## What are accommodations and modifications?

Accommodations and modifications are changes that we make to the curriculum with the goal of creating a more level playing field for all students. To put this in perspective, ask yourself if we would expect a student who is confined to a wheelchair to reach the curriculum standard in physical education. Could a student without legs run a mile in under seven minutes? We would not expect the same performance because the student has a physical disability. It's obvious to us that a physically disabled student will never be able to run a mile without prosthetics and practice. Just because the student cannot reach the standard and run a seven-minute mile, does that mean that the child with a disability should not have any physical education whatsoever or complete the mile in another way?

An accommodation levels the playing field so that all students have an opportunity to learn.

Since there are no federal standards for these two terms, some schools use them interchangeably, while other schools define accommodation as a support needed to gain access and modification as a change in standards. This change is made to support a student's learning style. In the case of a student with an IEP, modifications are decided by the planning and placement team, or IEP team.

## Why do students need accommodations and modifications?

When the IEP team determines that modifications are needed to level the playing field for a student, it is usually a result of extensive psychological and academic testing, as well as recommendations from the child's previous teachers due to the child's inability to succeed in "normal" circumstances. This may be due to a number of issues that can interfere with the processing of information and that adversely affect educational performance as defined by PL 94-142/IDEA.

## What is it like to have a cognitive disability?

Another question that comes up is, "What is it like to have a cognitive disability?" The best way to understand the answer to that question is to try the following timed task:

> Speak non-stop for one minute on the topic of your choice.
> However, you may not use any words that contain the letter N.

Ready? Go!

It is doubtful that very many readers found that exercise easy.

By deleting the letter N from your vocabulary, you were temporarily given a cognitive disability. It can't be seen from the outside, but it impairs ability. That's roughly equivalent to the experience of being learning disabled. Now that the exercise is over, you may return to using words with the letter N. However, a student with a cognitive processing problem must live with that disability every minute of every day.

As you were attempting the exercise, you may have become frustrated with how difficult it was and you may have chosen to skip it. Students with disabilities sometimes find it easier to quit than to be called lazy or labeled as "dumb."

Students with learning disabilities tend to have problems with memory and/or processing. They are easily embarrassed when they're called to answer a question, because they can't find the words to express themselves, or they give the answer that might have been correct three questions earlier. It's demoralizing to try and rarely succeed. That's why we teachers must level the playing field for students with cognitive problems. That's why modifications and accommodations are essential.

For more information, look for books and videos by Richard Lavoie. His F.A.T. City Workshop gave parents and teachers firsthand knowledge about the "frustration, anger and tension" that students with disabilities sometimes feel.

You may want to use this activity in your classroom if you want students to understand that you differentiate materials based on student needs. Some students think that the word "FAIR" means "SAME" or "EQUAL." Discussing why you give different items to different students might help alleviate sarcastic questions from some students when you are providing varied work. You might also address this issue through the lens of "bullying" - a difficult, albeit important discussion. Students with disabilities are the second most likely group to be bullied. Condescending comments on the work, which are meant to make these students feel inferior, are a form of verbal bullying.

## What is the difference between accommodations and modifications?

Accommodations create access. They are minor adjustments to allow the child access to the standards based curriculum.

Modifications occur when we begin to sift or adjust the curriculum standards based on what it is a particular child may need to know. A modification is a major change in expectations. The child is not held accountable to the same set of standards as the general education students.

## Do I have to modify and or accommodate?

If a student has a current IEP that contains accommodations/modifications, then those prescribed changes must be adhered to. Items outlined in the IEP are legal requirements. Any teachers or certified staff that work with the child with an IEP are accountable to those legal requirements.

This issue was decided definitively by a court case in 1995: Doe v. Withers:

http://www.wrightslaw.com/law/caselaw/case_Doe_Withers_Juryorder.html

Michael Withers was a high school teacher in West Virginia, and he refused to follow the modifications outlined in an IEP for a student in his history class. Even though the school's superintendent, principal, special education coordinator and other teachers had urged Mr. Withers to provide modifications as prescribed in the Individual Education Plan, Mr. Withers refused to comply. The parents decided to initiate their due process rights. The result was that Mr. Withers was found solely culpable for the neglect shown the student and ordered to personally pay $15,000 in damages.

For more information on legal precedent setting cases, please refer to the following web site:

http://www.kidstogether.org/right-ed.htm

## What if I do not agree with a modification?

Discuss your concerns with the child's case IEP manager. Until the outcome is decided, continue to follow prescribed modifications. The only place where a change in modifications can be made is during The IEP meeting. Anytime you have an IEP for a child in your classroom, it's your responsibility to ensure the plan is followed.

## Do I have to be part of the IEP meeting?

The IEP team is generally composed of the special education teacher, the student's parents and a member of the school administration. Also, a general education teacher if the child participates in any part of the general education curriculum, an individual who can interpret the instructional implications of evaluation results and when appropriate, the child. IDEA (§300.321)

Because of the importance placed on ensuring the IEP components are incorporated into the child's program, it is necessary to create some type of organization or tracking system to monitor a child's program and their progress in that program (progress monitoring or data collection/analysis.) On page 83, there is a reproducible chart for organizing and tracking IEPs. This list is not meant to represent all of the possible modifications, but only some of the more "popular" options used in public schools.

Each IEP must be developed individually, so it's important to be judicious when choosing modifications. As an example, some secondary educators get stuck thinking that there is the general education version of a test and a "special education" version. The illogical thinking is that the child with the IEP always receives the "special education" version. In this example, Individualization (the "I" in IEP) has been lost. What if the child is in a math class and is capable of doing the general education math, the disability being in the area of behavior — why would he or she need a modified test?

# Accommodation and Modification Categories

Accommodations and modifications aren't a one-size-fits-all endeavor. There are eight different categories in which we can accommodate/modify in order to teach and support a student in the general education classroom.

1. Behavior Management / Positive Behavioral Supports

   ➤ Behavior supports such as positive behavior and reinforcement programs, and response cost programs. These also may include behavioral assessments, intervention plans, and contingency plans with consequences.

2. Environment

   ➤ The environment includes items such as lighting, positioning of furniture, how the student can sit or stand, the use of space, the use of physical equipment, sound, music, and proximity to peers and adults.

3. Grading

   ➤ Specific parameters about how a child with a disability may be graded to determine competency and/or accountability.

4. Instructional Strategies

   ➤ Strategies that promote the child's acquisition of the required materials. These may include teaching strategies, learning strategies, use of materials, visuals, technology, lesson plan development, co-teaching, flexible groups, differentiated instruction, focus on learning styles, and a variety of other sound pedagogical practices.

5. Materials

   ➤ A variety of materials may be used to help the child acquire necessary knowledge or demonstrate competency in required curriculum/activities. May include use of very low tech (pencil grips) to very high tech (communication devices). Materials may also be instructional in nature (sticky notes, hand held white boards, etc.)

6. Organization

   ➤ Organization may refer to how the classroom is organized, or how lesson plans or materials are organized. It may also refer to "study skills" or academic requirements and related items such as the organization of notebooks and lockers, or other skills that fall under the heading of "executive function."

7. Assessments

   ➤ There are a variety of ways students can be assessed to demonstrate competency. This might refer to an assessment's timing, how it is administered, its alternative forms, or conditions under which it will or will not be given.

8. Expectations

   ➤ An outline of what expectations staff should have for students (Are they capable of following school rules? Should the student be accountable to an entire standard or just the "power" version of a standard? Should the student be expected to sit for an entire hour?) Expectations can be academic or behavioral. There are also expectations of both the student and the staff.

You can use these categories for reference as you develop your IEPs. You may want to consider creating a chart as an Excel file to help you track your modifications and accommodations and their usage. There are many online applications and programs that will help you create data charts and documents to simplify this process.

# Executive Function: Some Facts

The frontal and pre-frontal cortex regions are responsible for executive function processing.

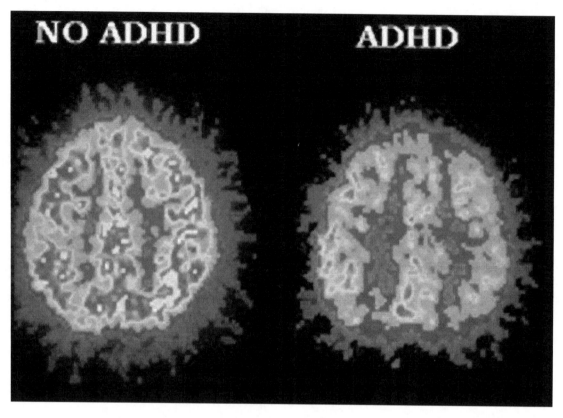

Executive function skills allow human beings to organize, plan, be aware of time and utilize working memory. Basic interaction and interpersonal skills may be negatively affected by deficits in this area.

Strategies to improve executive function should be taught explicitly, including teacher modeling and extensive practice. Strategies should be taught in a structured, systematic way and should address students' motivation and effort. Some of the skills needed by students with executive function disability are:

> Memorization

> Cognitive Flexibility

> Prioritizing

> Note-taking

> Self-monitoring

> Self-checking

> Organization

> Time Management

# Executive Function Skills

Some executive function skills that may affect a student's performance within the Common Core State Standards are listed below, along with goals for mastery of each skill.

Awareness
- ➢ To "tune in" their awareness so they can understand how information, events and their actions will impact their goals and objectives, both now and in the near future.

Forethought
- ➢ To predict the successful outcome of tasks and to know what a 'stop spot' looks like.

Inhibition
- ➢ To wait and control a reaction long enough to contemplate the outcomes of their choices.

Planning Skills
- ➢ To estimate time and sense the passage of time.
- ➢ To break down the steps for immediate tasks, nightly homework and long-term projects.

Ability to Shift
- ➢ To transition smoothly from one mental mindset and task to others.

Pacing
- ➢ To speed up or slow down within a given time frame
- ➢ To persist on tasks even if the tasks are difficult, boring or non-preferred.

Flexibility
- ➢ To consider multiple possible solutions to problems by considering the "grays" in a situation.

Tolerance
- ➢ To manage both expected and unexpected changes in plans, routines and rules, as well as uncertain or novel situations.

Organization
- ➢ To increase productivity.
- ➢ To create and maintain organizational systems for private and shared spaces and for personal belongings and school materials.

Create strategies and lesson plans to teach these skills explicitly within the general education classroom.

# How to Accommodate and Modify

Accommodations and modifications vary from task to task and from student to student. There is no set prescribed approach or method that should be used with consistency across all the different disability categories, instructional levels, academic and behavior levels. Much of what you need to do in this area is dictated by the child's individual profile (present level of academic and functional performance portion of the IEP). For instance, a student might need additional time to complete a lengthy assignment. Other students might need more profound supports such as a change in the curriculum.

It's not exclusively the students with disabilities who benefit from many of the accommodations. Some of the teaching strategies used in the special education process are just good differentiation strategies aimed at providing universal design and access of the curriculum for all students. One such example is the Chapter Outliner on page 52. This graphic organizer may be used as an instructional device to strengthen the note-taking process for all types of students. One good strategy to use in the differentiated classroom is to offer students an occasional structured choice. Students may be provided with the option of handing in a traditional outline using a prescribed Roman numeral method, or using the chapter outliner form as an acceptable means of completing the assignment.

In one case I worked on as a case manager, a hearing officer mandated that a high school student with an IQ of 45 should be fully included. We realized that no matter where he was placed, he would be behind the curriculum. We finally decided to place him in the honors history class. Our reasoning was that he was going to be behind academically no matter where we put him. The honors history class was a small class. Since there were no behavioral problems among the students, they provided appropriate role models. That allowed us to work on the student's social skills. It turned out to be an excellent decision. The students in the class were welcoming and kind. They actually created many of the modifications so the included student could participate in most of the academic activities. A few of the honors students created lasting true friendships with the included individual.

# Types of Modification

Depending on a student's abilities, there are different types of accommodation and modification that are appropriate. Below, the possibilities are organized into four types, although labeling them as Type 1 through 4 is not part of the official vocabulary of inclusion. Using types helps a teacher envision the difference between doing what is right for a child by providing just enough support versus the concerns of "watering down the curriculum" because too much support is offered.

Most secondary students participate in classrooms with Type 1 and Type 2 accommodations and modifications. Students with significant disabilities (usually in alternative testing systems for high stakes tests) might receive Type 3 and 4 modifications.

The IEP team determines the type of accommodations and modifications. Some students might need Type 2 modifications in one subject area, but only Type 1 in another area. For instance, a student might have a pronounced deficit in math, yet seem to function fine with just preferential seating and extra time in language arts. That should be a team decision during development of the IEP.

When an IEP indicates that we need to "modify tests," that could mean a number of things. For one student, a modified test might mean that the content of the test doesn't change, but the test is administered one section at a time so that it isn't overwhelming. For another student, a modification could mean fewer test questions. It's important to know which student needs what so that the curriculum isn't watered down unnecessarily.

Once students graduate, the information regarding their modifications is sealed. The only way that this information follows a student into the university is if the student chooses to self-identify. Students may request their confidential records from high school and present those at the university's disability office if they need accommodations. It becomes a self-identification or self-advocacy process.

After graduation from high school, the IDEA ends, but the accommodations allowed under section 504 continue throughout the rest of the student's educational life via post-secondary options, and then into the workforce. This is not true for Type 2 modifications and higher, because for many professions, content cannot be changed. For instance in order to become a nurse, there are rigid knowledge and skill requirements that are not negotiable. Beyond schooling, the person with disabilities is allotted continued special accommodations under the American with Disabilities Act, 1990, and protection under the Office of Civil Rights.

Every university is required to comply with students' valid accommodation requests. The Civil Rights Restoration Act of 1988 amended section 504 of the Rehabilitation Act of 1973 in part by stating that the term "program or activity" means: "all the operations of state or local government agencies and entities that receive funds from such agencies; entire colleges, universities or other postsecondary institutions, or public higher education systems; local educational agencies, systems of vocational education, or other school systems; corporations, partnerships or other private organizations that are principally engaged in providing education, health care, housing, social services or parks and recreation, or that receive federal financial assistance as a whole or any other organization that is established by two or more of the entities described above."

When I taught a teacher's course at a State University, there were students in the teacher preparation program who came to me with their section 504 disability plans. During exams, one of them required extended time and the other needed to use a word processor. I provided the tests in a secure envelope, and the tests were administered in compliance with the 504 prescribed fashion in the University disability office.

# Type 1 Accommodations

These are minor changes that do not affect the content standard. Educational outcomes and expectations are essentially the same as for general education students.

Type 1 accommodations: these allow access to the content in a unique manner, but still require a demonstration of competency in all of the prescribed materials.

Some examples of Type 1 accommodations are:

- Extended time on tests and quizzes
- Use of a word processor during a test
- Someone reads the test aloud
- A scribe or dictation to record information and answers
- Reduced number of test questions due to time factor (generally used when there are multiple practice opportunities of the same skill)
- Preferential seating
- Behavior modification techniques such as proximity control
- Access to a copy of teacher notes
- Use of a digital recorder
- Large print text
- Use of mnemonics
- Graphic organizers as teaching and learning tools
- Use displays
- Provide directions that are short and clear (using simple sentences)
- Give directions verbally and visually
- Color code
- Alternate text formats (i.e. digital)
- Extra texts for at-home use
- Provide tests one page at a time
- Prioritize test-taking according to points and time
- Use of sticky notes
- A question signal is developed between teacher and student
- Use of technology to aid access, such as MP3 players, digital recorders, technology boards, tablets, and smart phones

# Type 2 Modifications

With this type, we begin to change the content or the process. Based on the curriculum (what is it that we want all kids in the 8th grade to know, what is it we want all kids in 11th grade to know, or what is it that this particular course is offering), we determine which aspects of the standard are most important. If a student can't learn all the pieces, we might decide to hold him accountable to 70% of the standard. When we do that, it's called "sifting the curriculum" - choosing what it is we want a child to learn. That means that there are certain things that we purposely choose for him not to learn.

For example, when we modify the questions on a worksheet, instead of having him do every other problem, we might say that he's going to answer numbers 1, 3, 5, 8 and 12, because those teach to the standard that we're going to hold that student accountable for.

We modify with the standard in mind. The student may not reach the standard, but we always teach <u>to</u> the standard.

Here are examples of Type 2 modifications:

> A sampling of the easier examples
> Use of calculator
> Curriculum is prioritized; the student is only accountable for certain parts
> Peer helps with notebook organization, and provides any missing materials
> Content is altered slightly through materials or teacher expectation
> Grading is altered (See grading information on pages 192-195. Alternate grading procedures should be outlined in the IEP.)
> Grade is based on assigned work and not on curriculum standards
> Peer tutor
> Contract grading
> Curriculum sifting
> Cliff notes or a book with an alternate Lexile level
> Preview a movie on the same topic
> Homework expectations are altered
> A study guide is provided to the student a week before a test
> Special help for the subject area from teacher, tutor or peer
> Alternative assignments in area of strength are given to the student
> Assistive technology devices help the student demonstrate competency (i.e. word predicting programs and templates) in alternative ways.

# Type 3 Modifications

These are modifications we generally use for a child who participates in the general curriculum purely for the purposes of exposure. Generally, the progress of these students is measured by an alternate assessment at the district level. Teachers create and decide upon major changes in the student's participation in the curriculum. This is done through curriculum sifting. For example: the general education students complete a lab on the "Intersection of Tidal Zones and the Filtration of Pollutants." A Type 3 modification might consist of creating a poster to show the basic concepts of the water cycle.

This degree of modification constitutes a major change in the curriculum. The goal of these changes would be to provide students with exposure to the entire curriculum, while expecting mastery of only certain pieces. Examine the curriculum standard to determine the major concepts or "big ideas." Those are what the student will be held accountable for, and it may only be 30% of the curriculum. For instance in a social studies class, the student may only learn the most important concepts surrounding citizenship, but won't be expected to know all the steps regarding how a bill becomes a law.

Examples of Type 3 modifications:

> - Open note tests
> - Fill in the blank worksheet with page numbers to locate answers
> - Complete examples whose answers can be found in the back of the book
> - Complete hands-on projects (using a strength area) instead of a writing assignment
> - Parallel content book at a lower reading level (these are available in children's sections of libraries and book stores as well as the English-as-a-second-language sections)
> - Complete only the easy examples on the page
> - Have student work with a high ability partner and submit one paper together
> - In cooperative groups, assign the student to be the materials manager or timekeeper
> - Give the student a study guide with page numbers or answers
> - Have student fill in a graphic organizer instead of writing a paragraph
> - Answer only sifted questions

# Type 4 Modifications

This degree of modification is known as a parallel curriculum, with the goal of having the student participate in the curriculum in a general way and also focusing on the social skills needed for future success in the community and on the job. The student is not responsible for the curricular materials as presented, but participates academically through a parallel curriculum that focuses on similar concepts related to life skills, as deemed appropriate. The alternative materials the student completes have only a basic relationship to the classroom requirements. Here are a couple of examples:

> Instead of practicing inference skills with a classroom novel, the student predicts, "What do you think will happen?" when he does not pick up his trash from around his desk when asked.

> While the other students are working on sketch notes to sequence the main events in a story, the student with a Type 4 modification is given a picture sequence of his day to put in order.

Type 4 modifications would apply to students who are very cognitively challenged. For example, one of the curriculum standards is proficiency in computer skills by the time of graduation. For a student in a wheelchair with no use of his arms except for a bit of elbow movement, proficiency might consist of using technology to turn on a switch. We're always teaching to the standard, but the expectations in this example are nowhere near that. What we teach that student relates back to a life skill or a practical skill.

Type 4 modifications might include:

> Have the student highlight terms in a handout that relate to basic life skills
> Group the student with peers who are good behavior role models and grade the student based on how well those behaviors are exhibited in class
> Assign the student to call a classmate every homework night to remind him or her to do homework
> The student collects and passes out papers in the classroom, appropriately greeting each classmate by name
> The teacher identifies from one to a few key concepts per unit and the student completes parallel work around the concept(s)
> Grade is based on a grading contract that focuses on appropriate participation and use of skills such as following directions
> Grade is based on a behavior contract
> Student audits the course or takes the course as pass/fail
> Student uses technology to create his or her own project
> The teacher underlines a few key words on the board surface and the student only copies the key words to participate in note-taking. (These may be key academic terms, or perhaps high frequency words the student needs to practice writing.)
> Other students in the class that need oral reading practice take turns reading to the student with Type 4 modification needs (round robin style).

# Accommodation Planner

| Date | Standards/Objectives: |
|---|---|
| **What will students be able to Know, Understand and Do?**<br><br>K<br><br><br>U<br><br><br>D | Differentiation: |
| IEP Goals to Consider: | How student will respond: (TAPS)<br><br>Total Class Response<br><br><br>Alone<br><br><br>Pairs<br><br><br>Small Cooperative Groups |

## How do I keep track of all those modifications?

A general secondary education teacher might have 120+ students throughout the day, thirty of which have IEPs. Each one of those students with disabilities might need twenty modifications. That's a lot of accommodations and modifications to keep track of. The Modification Tracker on pages 82-83 is designed to help you organize your accommodations and modifications so that you can efficiently and effectively manage all of your student's needs.

## TEACHING TIP

### How to create a modification tracker

You may choose to use the reproducible on page 83 or you might create the same type of graphic organizer electronically. Here are some tips:

- Create the organizers by CLASS (not by case manager or by alphabetical listing of all of the students with disabilities).

- If you choose to use a hard copy version of the list, place it in a folder and mark the folder confidential. Remember to store the folder in the confidential manner prescribed by your school system (i.e. store it in a locked file cabinet located in a locked room).

- Create one color coded folder per class you teach (Period 3 is a yellow folder, Period 4 is a blue folder, etc.). Each list inside the folder contains only the names of the students for that class period.

## What goes on the Modification Tracker?

The first column is designated for the student's name and also contains the initials of the case manager (CM). In the example, it is the special education teacher assigned to monitor that student's IEP. The number indicates the type of modification that the student requires. The remaining categories are arranged with the same groupings as on the modifications page.

Take a look at the sample. The first entry is Eric, T-1, SK – meaning that Eric would receive Type 1 accommodations, and since I was his case manager, those are my initials.

As a special educator, I would fill out this form and then sit down with the general educator to review the information. I found General Education teachers to be very appreciative of the information that was organized succinctly in this easy-to-read format. It helped the General education teacher, or the co-teacher teacher, keep track of the support needed by each student with an IEP. The form is very easy to use. For example, if the teacher intended to give a quiz, he would scan the column for tests and quizzes to understand that:

- Eric only needs a study guide
- Paul requires Type 3 modifications, which means a modified test, as well as extra time.
- Son is going to take the standard test, but he needs a little extra time, and he needs the test administered orally.

Because of the individual needs of various students, there isn't one modification that's appropriate for all. Giving a modified test to a student who only needs a little extra time would amount to unnecessarily watering down the curriculum. When it comes to accommodations and modifications, there is a lot of room for professional interpretation This chart helps us clarify some of the ambiguity that can be caused by some terms such as "modified tests."

## SPECIAL STRATEGY

### Managing Your Modifications
Physical and virtual files

Managing some of these modifications can be a real issue, and there is a further problem with reinventing the wheel each time a change is needed. To prevent duplicate work and wasted time, keep a copy of all the modifications that you make. If they are on paper, start a modification file drawer for your department. For instance, the whole science department would have access to all of the modifications for biology, anatomy, marine science, etc.

If you make modifications digitally, start an online file cabinet. Many school districts offer shared cyberspace where teachers can post and organize digital files. Eventually, the department will have a comprehensive collection of modifications. This is especially helpful for the general education teacher, who can now access the information without having to seek out extra help or spend time developing modifications from scratch.

## Cumulative vs. Confidential

When teachers collect information on students, it will either be filed as a general record in the cumulative or "cume" file, or in the confidential file that contains sensitive information such as the IEP and the minutes from team meetings. Legally, the confidential file must be kept locked with restricted access. Any information that discusses or discloses the identify of a disability must be kept in a confidential format. Therefore, leaving IEPs or copies of modification lists on teachers' desks is not acceptable.

# Modification Tracker

| Student and CM | Material/ Books | Test/ Quizzes | Grading | Orgnztn | Envrnmt | B. Mod/ Support | Instruct. Strategy |
|---|---|---|---|---|---|---|---|
| * Eric – (T-1) SK | | Study Guide | No spelling penalty | assign notebook partner | | | Use mnemonics |
| Rachel – (T-2) SK | Modified Worksheets | | | | Pref. Seating | Proximity Control | Concrete Examples + Graphic Organ. |
| Paul – (T-3) VL | Modified Worksheets | Extra time | No Spell penalty + Modified grades | | | | Modified Content |
| Venisha (T-2) VL | Modified Worksheets | | | | | | Use mnemonics + graphic organizers |
| Son (T-1) NC | | Extra time Oral Testing | | | | | Modified Notes Vocabulary Cards |
| Matteo (T-3) NC | Calculator | Test Study Guide + Extra time | Base grade on ability | | Positive Reinforce. Behavior Contract | Break b/t tasks + Pref. Seat. near tchr. | Use manipulat Concrete Examples |
| Lindsay (T-1) NC | Extra set of books at home | Portion out tests | | Notebook Checks Bi-Weekly | allow breaks for Movement | | Hight light + Mult-Sens. Visual Reinforce. |
| Fred (T-1) NC | Large print | Extra space for writing | | Study Outline 1 week in advance | Seating near board | | Use overhead for examples |

* type of modification          CM= case manager

# Modification Tracker

| Student and CM | Material/ Books | Test/ Quizzes | Grading | Orgnztn | Envrnmt | B. Mod/ Support | Instruct. Strategy |
|---|---|---|---|---|---|---|---|
|  |  |  |  |  |  |  |  |
|  |  |  |  |  |  |  |  |
|  |  |  |  |  |  |  |  |
|  |  |  |  |  |  |  |  |
|  |  |  |  |  |  |  |  |
|  |  |  |  |  |  |  |  |
|  |  |  |  |  |  |  |  |
|  |  |  |  |  |  |  |  |

# Confidentiality and Creating Acceptance for Differentiation Among Students

Because it is a violation of protocol to identify a student as having a disability to his or her peers, it can sometimes be tricky to address classroom questions about why a student is receiving a different test from everyone else, or why one student has a study guide with words filled in, whereas everyone else has to fill in the blanks.

One solution is to hand out tests or study guides that have the same first page or that have a uniform cover page. Another solution is to tell students that there are several different versions of the test (A, B and C). The teacher is the only one that knows that A is for general education students, B is for a particular student that has Type 1 accommodations, and C is for the student with weak grapho-motor and process writing skills, and who receives Type 2 modifications including extra writing space and shortened essay questions to be answered in graphic organizer format. The class will most likely assume that the reason for there being several types of test is to prevent cheating.

By the time students reach the secondary level, they tend to know who the students are that need extra help because they've shared classes with them. At times, teachers worry about what to say to students who complain that it's not fair for another student to receive different materials. If the issue of fairness needs to be addressed, you could have the students engage in the "No Letter N" activity on page 65. Another terrific resource to help everyone understand that diversity is not an issue related solely to culture or race is the F.A.T. City video workshop by Richard Lavoie. After 45 minutes of sensitizing activities, kids leave with an understanding of what it's like to have academic challenges, and they realize why modifications are important. These exercises help students construct a new definition of the word "fair."

Our constitution does not allow us to discriminate based on race, religion, gender, or handicapping condition. Academic diversity exists and needs to be treated with respect. When it comes to delivering education tailored to each student's requirements and abilities, fair is the other four-letter F-word.

# We've Always Done It This Way

We often get stuck doing the same things the same way, year after year.

For a very good example of how traditions can become entrenched, consider the size of the Space Shuttle's booster rockets. These solid rocket boosters, or SRBs, are shipped by train from the factory to the launch site. The size of the SRBs was ultimately determined by the width of the train tracks, which in the United States is 4 ft 8.5 inches.

That is an exceedingly odd number for a rail gauge, and it leads to the question, "Why is that measurement used?" The answer is that it's because that's the way they built the train tracks in England, and it was English ex-patriots who designed our railroads. Why did the English build them that way? Because the first rail lines were built by the same people who built the pre-railroad tramways and those were the measurement specifications they used. And why did early English road engineers use that gauge? Because the people who built the tramways used the same jigs and tools that they used for building wagons, which used the same wheel spacing. Why did they use that odd wheel spacing? Because if you tried to use a different wheel spacing, wagon axles risked breaking because of the deep ruts in the old roads, so wagons were designed to travel in the ruts. And who built those old roads? The first long-distance roads in Europe were built by Imperial Rome for the benefit of their legions. The roads have been used ever since and the ruts – the initial ruts which everyone else had to match for fear of destroying their wagons - were first made by Roman war chariots. Since the chariots were made by and for Imperial Rome, they were all fabricated with the same wheel spacing. Thus we have the answer to the original question. The size of the Space Shuttle's rockets was determined by the US standard railroad gauge, 4 feet 8.5 inches, which derives from the original specification for the Imperial Roman army war chariot.

Bureaucracies rarely innovate, so the next time you're handed specifications and you wonder what horse's ass came up with them, you may be exactly right. Because the Imperial Roman chariots were constructed to be just wide enough to accommodate the back ends of two warhorses.

In the educational setting, policies are set in stone just because we've done things a certain way for 30 years. As a point in fact, consider that the desks in classrooms are almost always organized into rows. Whether or not that is the best seating arrangement for a group of students, janitors chose the arrangement because the distance between rows was the same measurement as the head of the push broom.

Sometimes, it's wise to think out of the box and question our practices. When we imagine how we might do things a little differently, we are able to accommodate various needs.

# The Four Types of Modification in Practice

Here is an example of how the different types of accommodations and modifications might look when applied to a reading assignment from Jack London's book *White Fang*.

General education: Circle one of *White Fang*'s quotes below. Write your initial thoughts, observations and ideas about the quotation, explain what it has to do with the story.

For a Type 1 accommodation, you might chunk the instructions because many students with disabilities have a hard time following more than two-part directions. Leave plenty of white space and bullet the directions as follows:

- ❖ Circle the quotes below from the last chapter of *White Fang*.

- ❖ Write your initial thoughts, observations and ideas about the quotation on a graphic organizer.

- ❖ Explain what it has to do with the story of *White Fang*.


For a Type 2 modification, use simpler language. It may also be necessary to provide raised line writing paper (tactile paper that stops a pencil from traveling beyond the line), because students with grapho-motor issues find it difficult to write in a blank space.

1. Pick your favorite part of the last chapter of *White Fang*.

2. Copy that part on the lines below.

_____

_____

3. Tell why it is your favorite part.

_____

_____

A Type 3 modification still has the student do some problem solving, while also connecting the reading material to life skills:

Draw a picture of a time when you let other people lead you in the wrong direction, and you got into trouble because of them.




Write or dictate what is happening in the picture:

_____

_____

Write or dictate what could you have done differently?

_____

_____


A Type 4 modification might be for the student with communication issues who is confined to a wheelchair. One example would be:

- ❖ The classroom paraprofessional holds up two pictures.
- ❖ The student has to decide which is right and which is wrong.
- ❖ The student points to the image that is wrong.

# Prioritizing Content

"How do I know what to hold a student accountable for?"

The best way to pick and choose what's important is determined by the subject matter being taught. Ask yourself, "What part of this is important for all students to know?"

Our content is arranged in the following way:

- Material we want ALL students to know

- Material that we want MOST students to understand

- Material consisting of extension activities: SOME students will relate to the material that we're teaching and these activities will take learning to the next level.

What is it that we need all kids to know? Whatever that standard is, it becomes your point of reference. Determine what accommodation or modification a student will need, and reference the modification list to determine the type.

Try the following:

1. Determine what content objectives you will be teaching

2. Determine the type of modifications the student will need (Type 1, 2, 3, 4, or a combination)

3. Now pick the objectives the student will be responsible for **learning**, which the student will only have **exposure** to, and the ones which the student **will not be accountable for**, and which objectives will require **parallel or alternate materials** (e.g. projects).

4. Now that you have determined the focus area(s), you have a premise from which to select work to modify. See the example science unit outline on page 90. If, for example, you are asking a student to answer questions on the "citric acid cycle" but not "the electron transport chain (ETC)", then you may eliminate questions on "ETC" on the student's homework and only require the student to answer the questions on the citric acid cycle. On a quiz, you would eliminate the questions on "ETC" and only grade the ones on the citric acid cycle.

5. Implement the IEP recommended accommodations/modifications. If "modified tests and quizzes" is a recommendation, then by eliminating items the student is responsible for, you have modified the quiz.

One theory that forms the foundation of inclusion is that it is possible to help a student master information in order to achieve a proposed standard, as long as one teaches to the child's strength.

The Biochemical Pathways of Respiration on page 90 represents a unit outline for a high school science class.

One of the students in that class was Paul, who was on the cross-country running team at school. As you can see on the sample Modification Tracker on page 82, Paul received Type 3 modifications.

Keeping our eyes on the standard, the general education teacher and I examined our expectations for Paul's participation in the course, and what was important for him to learn. We decided that we would hold him accountable for numbers 4, 5, 6 and 12 on the unit outline. For number 5, he would demonstrate competency in that area by developing a 3-D diagram. We asked him to construct a mobile that demonstrated various aspects of respiration. Our assumption was that he would do well because as a long-distance runner, he could relate to respiration.

# BIOCHEMICAL PATHWAYS OF RESPIRATION

- There are three steps to the breakdown of glucose: glycolysis, the citric acid cycle, and the electron transport chain.
- First part is a lot like fermentation. What was the intermediate? (Pyruvic acid)
- This step is anaerobic, and makes about 10% of the ATP. (Make a chart-Step, ATP produced. Keep tally)

1. Glucose forms pyruvic acid, and releases 2 molecules of ATP.
2. Pyruvic acid enters...? (Mitochondrion)
3. Pyruvic acid breaks down to form $CO_2$ and a 2-carbon molecule called ACETIC ACID
4. $CO_2$ leaves as waste, acetic acid attaches to a carrier molecule and enters the CITRIC ACID CYCLE
5. What does cycle mean? Begins and ends with the same compound. First molecule formed is CITRIC ACID when the 2-carbon acetic acid attaches to a 4-carbon molecule.
6. Citric acid is broken down in a series of reactions.
7. Each time 2 $CO_2$ are lost, another 2 C acetic acid on, off, on, off, on, off. (cycle) The purpose of this is to break 3 C pyruvic acid into 3 molecules of $CO_2$.
8. How many molecules of $CO_2$ are produced from one molecule of glucose? (6) How many times must this cycle for each molecule of glucose? (6) How many ATP are produced? (6)
9. With each cycle, high-energy electrons are given off. These enter the ELECTRON TRANSPORT CHAIN.
10. Not to waste anything, the high-energy electrons are saved for later. (dessert) THIS is where it gets good. Electrons are picked up by electron carriers and taken to inner membrane of mitochondria.
11. Electrons are passed from one coenzyme to another, energy is given off. (fig. 6-8, like water spilling out of the bucket) The energy makes an ATP molecule. By the time an electron reaches the end of the chain, it has lost most of its energy. (30 ATP are produced)

- We said this is aerobic respiration. Where is the oxygen?
- Electrons at the end of the chain have to be removed. These electrons are picked up by oxygen. We also said that 4 Hydrogen atoms are produced. What is 4H +2O? $2H_2O$. The other waste product.
- Oxygen clears the debris so that the system can keep moving. Oxygen is the body's janitor. Without it, the entire process would get cluttered and just down.

12. Oxygen cleans up the junk.

# CONTENT MODIFICATIONS

# Reading Strategies

There are strategies we can use that will help students become better readers. However, we won't know what strategy to use until we determine the student's current reading level. This can be accomplished by using the readability formulas on pages 93 and 94.

Formula 1 is a quick readability test for a student to take. This helps a teacher determine if the text materials are an appropriate match for the student's independent reading level.

---

### Determining Independent Reading Levels

Give the student a 200-word passage from a text.

If the student can read:

98% of more of the words = Independent level (the level for homework)

95% - 97% of the words = Instructional level (the level for classroom materials)

94% or less of the words = Frustration level (consider modifying the readability of the material or use alternate materials)

---

Formula 2 assesses the readability of a textbook. A text might appear to be written at an 8th or 9th grade level, when it fact it could be for a 6th grade or 11th grade level. SMOG stands for "some measure of gobbledegook" and will allow you to quickly determine whether a text is appropriate for your students.

Here is a list of strategies and practices that can improve your students' comprehension and retention:

> Sticky note strategy (page 96)
> Side-by-side books and abridged copies
> Use of bullets
> Use of simple sentences
> Use of white space and graphic organizers
> Bold and highlight key words
> Define difficult terms
> Peer buddy readers
> Volunteer readers for community service credit
> Chunking reading material using symbols or dots
> Focused reading strategies (eliminate amount)

Use the following two readability formulas to determine if the content reading is too difficult for your student(s).

## Readability Formula 1

Cloze Readability Test

This very simple procedure is applicable to all grade levels and will give you a readability estimate.

1. Select a passage from your classroom materials of 250-300 words.

2. Retype the passage on a blank sheet. Type the first sentence intact. Reproduce subsequent sentences, deleting every fifth word and inserting a standard blank (about ten spaces long on a size 12 font). Type the last sentence intact.

3. Distribute the reproduced passage with deletions to the student. Students are to fill in each blank word with the word they think was deleted. No specific time limit is needed.

4. To evaluate, count only the insertions that exactly match the deleted word. Ignore spelling errors of correct words.

5. 40% correct or below = material is too difficult for student (frustration reading level)
   41 – 59% correct = student's instructional level
   60% or better = the student can handle the material independently.

Sample paragraph: The content modifications depend on the student's ability to read the content material. The first thing you _____ do is to test the _____ readability level. From there _____ can determine the type _____ modifications that will be _____. This is how you decide how to proceed with modifications.

# Readability Formula 2

SMOG Grading

"Some measure of gobbledygook." This formula looks at the number of syllables in the words of a passage. This is especially good for content that has a lot of polysyllabic vocabulary. The teacher analyzes the content itself to determine if it meets a student's needs.

1. Count ten sentences near the beginning of the text to be used. Count ten more in the middle of the text. Then count ten near the end of the text.

2. Using the thirty sentences selected above, count every word of three or more syllables. Any string of numbers or numerals beginning and ending with a space or punctuation mark should be counted if you can make out at least three syllables when you read the text aloud. If a polysyllabic word is repeated, count each repetition.

3. Determine the square root of the number of polysyllabic words counted.

4. Add 3 to the square root. This gives you a SMOG grade, which is the reading grade that a student should have reached to fully understand the text.

For example:                         No. of polysyllabic words

Beginning 10 sentences:                        7
Middle 10 sentences:                          10
End 10 sentences:                           + 8
Total:                                        25

Square root is 5

5+3=8

Readability for this text is 8th grade.

# MS Word Readability Formula

Microsoft Word contains a Flesh-Kincaid readability index that rates your content according to grade level. To activate this function, go to "Spelling and Grammar." At the bottom of the dialogue box is a button for "Options." Clicking it will bring up a window with a number of possibilities, including "show readability index."

To use the function, highlight a block of text and then select "Spelling and Grammar." Word will check the grammar first. When that's done and a window asks whether you want to check the rest of the document, click "no." At that point, Word displays a window with various statistics. The readability grade level is at the bottom of the window.

If you realize that you have inadvertently written a college level test for your 8th grade class, you can easily adjust the reading level downward by replacing multi-syllabic words with simpler synonyms, and by adding more periods to break up complex sentences.

Here is an example from H.G. Wells' *The Invisible Man:*

*The stranger came early in February, one wintry day, through a biting wind and a driving snow, the last snowfall of the year, over the down, walking from Bramblehurst railway station, and carrying a little black portmanteau in his thickly gloved hand.*

## Readability Statistics

| Counts | |
|---|---|
| Words | 42 |
| Characters | 210 |
| Paragraphs | 1 |
| Sentences | 1 |

| Averages | |
|---|---|
| Sentences per Paragraph | 1.0 |
| Words per Sentence | 42.0 |
| Characters per Word | 4.8 |

| Readability | |
|---|---|
| Passive Sentences | 0% |
| Flesch Reading Ease | 41.3 |
| Flesch-Kincaid Grade Level | 12.0 |

OK

# Reading Comprehension: Sticky Note Strategy

The Sticky Note strategy works well for students who need help answering reading comprehension questions.

➢ First, begin by pre-reading - giving an overview of the words and graphics that will be encountered in the text.

➢ Have the student locate and read the comprehension questions.

➢ Ask the student to write each question on a separate sticky note, and line them up in front of the book. (If you have five questions, you will have five sticky notes.)

➢ Have the student read in manageable chunks: to the end of the line, paragraph or page.

➢ Then ask the student to match the question on the sticky note to the answer in the book. For example, one of the questions might be, "What are the three bones of the ear called?" As the student reads and encounters the words "stirrup, hammer and anvil," the sticky note is placed at that point in the text. The student continues to read until all of the questions on sticky notes have been matched to the answers.

This strategy prevents students from skimming for the questions' keywords, then copying the sentence before and after (and praying that's the answer). This technique encourages students to actually do the reading. In the case of Type 1 accommodations, students copy down the questions and answers in their notes. This becomes an invaluable independent study guide for a test.

Sticky notes can be a bit expensive, but there are sticky note glue sticks and rollers available at office supply stores, which transform regular paper into sticky notes.

---

Sticky Note Strategy Outline

1. Identify what you need to read and complete pre-reading activities.

2. Locate and read the questions of the passage.

3. Put one question on a sticky note.

4. Line your questions up in front of you.

5. Chunk your reading into sections.

6. Read your section and match the question to the answer

7. Place the post-it note with the question on it by the answer.

8. Review the questions.

9. Begin reading the next chunk and repeat the process.

---

# SPECIAL STRATEGY

## Quick reading strategy: Closed Captions

Reading is something that is taught in elementary school, not as much at the secondary level. And yet, secondary school teachers may have students that struggle with reading.

Parents often want to know what they can do to help their teenagers who are still having difficulty reading. One easy strategy is to have the parents turn on the closed captioning option and mute the volume when the child is watching TV. Closed captions are a transcription of the audio portion of a television program for the hearing impaired and they appear at the bottom of the screen. They can facilitate learning how to read, even if it's just for half an hour a day.

When showing a video in the classroom, closed captions can help those students who have visual and auditory processing issues connect with what's going on in the video, because then they can see some key words as they move across the screen – as long as the screen is large enough to accommodate the type.

A closed caption option is available on the iPad tablet. You will find the built-in access to turn on closed captioning by going into:

> > settings
> > videos
> > closed captioning

# Focused Writing With RAFTs

The RAFTs technique is a system to help students understand their role as a writer, the audience they will address, the varied formats for writing, and the expected content (Santa, 1988).

> **R**ole of the writer. Who are you as the writer? Are you King Henry? A surfer? A homeless person who plays music in a subway to make money? A professional athlete? A dog?

> **A**udience. To whom are you writing? Is your audience a group of protesters? A family member? Your Pastor? Magazine subscribers? A hiring agent?

> **F**ormat. What form will the writing take? Is it a letter? A classified ad? A speech? A poem? An argument?

> **T**opic. What's the subject or the point of this piece? Is it to persuade your principal to allow you to graduate despite your grades? To plead for a new car on your 16th birthday? To recruit people to join the fundraising 5K run for the child with leukemia?

> **S**trong verb. Leap off to a quick start with an action verb that will ensnare your reader's attention.

## What Is The Purpose?

The purpose of RAFTs is to provide students an opportunity to approach writing assignments with creativity and purpose.

Generally, RAFTs are written from a viewpoint different from the student's, to another audience rather than the teacher, and in a form different from the ordinary theme. Therefore, students are encouraged to think and respond creatively as they connect to newly learned information through their imagination.

# Teaching Writing Using RAFTs
## Workshop Model

**Step one:**

Explain to the students how all writers have to consider various aspects before every writing assignment including role, audience, format, and topic. Tell them that they are going to structure their writing around these elements. Supply students with a list of the various forms of writing and the components they are to include. Have students create a checklist of these components BEFORE they begin writing.

**Step two:**

Display an exemplar completed RAFTs example on the general teaching board of the classroom, and discuss the key elements as a class. Have students mark up and note key components on their copy of the exemplar using highlighters, sticky notes or other interactive devices (example: iannotate on their iPads).

**Step three:**

Demonstrate, model, and "think aloud" another sample RAFTs. When demonstrating "think aloud" to students with disabilities, it is always important that the teacher demonstrate using the word "I." An example of what you might say to your students: "I think I will have my audience be a bunch of Hollywood producers looking for their next script. I will try and convince them that I have the next blockbuster story, so they should invest in my writing."

**Step four:**

Ask students to pair up to complete a RAFTs assignment on a chosen topic. After they brainstorm their approach, have them take turns writing and dictating alternate paragraphs. Next, have them critique their writing using the components they set out in step one.

**Step five:**

Provide the pairs with assistance as needed, such as mini conferences with each pair. Then have some of the pairs share their completed assignments with the class.

**Step six:**

After students become more proficient in developing this style of writing, have them generate RAFTS assignments on their own based on current topics studied in class.

## Assessment and Evaluation

A variety of rubrics exist to rate your RAFTs. Use the phrase "RAFT writing rubric" in your Internet search.

# RAFT

| Role | Audience | Format | Topic |
|------|----------|--------|-------|
|      |          |        |       |
|      |          |        |       |
|      |          |        |       |
|      |          |        |       |
|      |          |        |       |

### Side-by-Side Books / Abridged Books / Alternative Books

A side-by-side book can act as bridge material for children who have reading problems. Shakespeare's plays are often published in side-by-side format, with the original text on one side and a modern English version on the opposite page.

Some books also come with an audio CD, which helps students with their reading skills because they can follow along with the spoken word. See the list on pages 107-108 for websites that publish books in alternative formats.

### Audio-taped textbooks

In this era of mp3 files, many books are available as audio recordings.

Please see "Learning Ally" at http://www.learningally.org (formerly Readings for the Blind and Dyslexic) to see if your student qualifies for free subscription of pre-recorded books.

### SPECIAL STRATEGY

### Special Recordings

There may be specific texts you would like to have recorded in a particular way; for instance, to include pre-reading before each chapter. In that case, you might ask a student group to record some scripts for you.

Many students are looking for opportunities to complete community service hours for various school and club requirements. Have volunteers read textbooks into digital recorders, create powerpoints to outline textbook information, highlight key information in a textbook for you, and a variety of other tasks to help you grow your access materials.

## Choral Reading

Oral reading consists of each student in turn reading a passage out loud. Students with reading difficulties often anticipate what sections they will have to read and practice their assigned section in order to sound fluent when reading in front of their peers. This often leads to the following scenario: the student is so overwhelmed with silently practicing the reading beforehand, he does not hear what his classmates are reading. Following his performance, his feelings of relief may be so intense that he fails to pay attention to the text read by others.

Choral reading alleviates this problem because the entire group reads at the same time. Generally, the teacher leads off the reading and sets a pace that is slower than usual. After the group begins to read in unison, the teacher stops reading in order to survey the students. It is a good idea to encourage students with disabilities to track the reading with their finger, the edge of a ruler, index card or some other device and mouth the words if they are insecure about their skills.

When everyone reads the same passage at once, comprehension is increased because the information is read with fluency. Students with reading difficulties are able to mouth their way through the words without being embarrassed. Difficult words are pronounced correctly, and the student often gains vocabulary understanding when words are correctly pronounced and read fluently in context.

## KU Center for Research on Learning

The University of Kansas has a Center for Research on Learning, which is a terrific resource for data-based reading, writing, and skill acquisition interventions. The center suggests many strategies that make use of an eight-step method for teaching at-risk learners the skills they need to achieve academic independence.

http://www.kucrl.org/research

# Comprehension Strategies for the Secondary Student and Specially Designed Instruction / Meeting IEP Goals within the General Education Environment

## Paraphrasing

Teach students to find the main idea in a passage, along with one or two details. The main idea and details are then combined into a single sentence in the student's own words. Have the students draw lines or create stopping points on a text page by using little sticky flags. Students read the assigned chunk of material (usually a manageable paragraph or a page in a small novel), and then create a paraphrase of key ideas from that chunk. The average textbook is generally chunked into three or four sections per page. Use the Paragraph Summary organizer on page 53.

Another example of paraphrasing is the use of Sketch Notes (see pages 115-117). The teacher chunks the lesson materials into small manageable pieces, stopping every three to four minutes to allow students to create quick sketches and key words to remember the presented material.

Embed these strategies into the student's regular routine. For example, as an alternate classwork or homework assignment, have the student summarize key paragraphs in a section instead of answering questions on a worksheet. Create a graphic organizer to aid the student in this approach.

## Summarizing

Combined with paraphrasing, summarizing is another key comprehension strategy. After the student has completed the paraphrasing activity on a page or section, the student then combines the paraphrases into a three-to-four sentence paragraph that summarizes the key points from that section.

Have students first practice this skill orally before they respond in writing. By gaining oral fluency with the process, students with disabilities have an easier time translating the information into written language. For example, pair up students and have them buddy read. After each paragraph, the buddies take turns paraphrasing. At the end of the exercise, the pair works to create one summary, which one of them records <u>after</u> it has been expressed orally.

To use with Sketch Notes, students create a small paragraph on the back of the Sketch Notes worksheet.

## Visualization Strategy

Please see the Visualization Lesson on pages 35-37. To boost visual comprehension, it may be important to first build visual memory in students with disabilities.

For students with disabilities at the secondary level, there seems to be a correlation between a lack of good visual motor memory and poor spelling skills. These students cannot envision the correct spelling in their visual memory, nor does automatic muscle memory take over to produce appropriate letter sequences. It is important for students with disabilities to develop visual memory and visual comprehension skills because the lack of visualization not only affects spelling, but comprehension and writing skills as well. Students often report their writing lacks detail because their "mind's eye" cannot envision what those details might be.

This is another area where developing the oral language through a paired buddy system may be your best first step. Have students complete the activity below - orally first. Once they are comfortable with the oral process, then have them move to drawing and writing. A modification may be for students to record the visual comprehension techniques with a digital recorder, smart phone or tablet as an alternative to a written product submission.

If there is visual content, such as a graphically described novel or scientific concept, then it may be appropriate to use a visual imagery strategy. This can also be an effective tool in social studies when describing events with strong visuals, such as wars, or in mathematics for describing application problems. For content that does not lend itself to visualization, you may substitute the use of symbols to represent a concept. For example, in a poem that contains the concept of the "colors of love," a blue heart could stand for "brokenhearted."

Have students read a section of a text. At the end of a paragraph, ask them to sketch out a description of the setting. For instance, if the text is set in a jungle, then students might draw palm trees and perhaps a snake or two lurking in the undergrowth. Ask them to embellish the scene so that they create a vision of where they are.

One way to practice visual imagery is to have the students create a chart with six sections, one for each of the six senses. "What is the look, sound, touch, taste, smell and feeling of the place?" One answer might be: "The jungle has giant palm trees with rough bark encircled by flowering vines. The aroma of the flowers is so sweet, you can almost taste it. I hear a snake hissing nearby, and I feel the eyes of unseen animals tracking my every move."

## Self-Questioning

As students work their way through a text, they pause at the end of each paragraph and ask themselves a question using one of the seven question words: who, what, when, where, which, why or how. The students then write their questions on sticky notes and place the notes in the book in one color (for example, on a small yellow sticky note, the student writes: Why did the weather change so quickly? What does the approaching storm mean?)

Have the students create questions using the low level question words (who, what, when, where, which) only once or twice. Have them use the higher level question words (why, how) multiple times. Also encourage the student to use the phrases, "I wonder..." and "What if..."

## Predictions and Inferences

Once the student/pair has created a question, they make a prediction on a different colored sticky and place it next to their original question: "I think the approaching storm symbolized that something bad is about to happen."

After completing the reading, students go back and rate their predictions as to whether they were right or wrong. They place a plus or a minus on their prediction sticky. By interacting paragraph-by-paragraph, comprehension is improved.

## Mark it up!

There are many technology apps that can be used to mark up text with a stylus, a finger, highlights, bolding. Consider how you can use technology to mark up a text.

It is possible to purchase USED copies of classroom books from online vendors. The least expensive copies that are advertised as "has highlights and notes" turn out to be the most useful for the student who needs additional reading support.

## Buddy reading

It can be helpful to pair up non-readers with students who need to practice reading. The non-reader hears the material, and the reader gets a boost of self-esteem because he's helping someone else for a change instead of people always helping him.

# TEACHING TIP

**Create Highlight Cards**

Laminate 3 x 5 index cards. Place a variety of colored sticky flags or pieces of highlighting tape on the card. As students read a text, they might use blue flags to highlight key vocabulary words and place red flags next to important concepts. When the section is no longer being studied, the student removes the flags and highlighting tape and returns them to the 3 x 5 laminated card. This allows the materials to be reused.

# Assistive Technology Tools: Making Reading Accessible *

| SOLO | http://www.donjohnston.com/products/solo/index.html |
|---|---|
| WYNN | http://www.freedomscientific.com/LSG/products/wynn.asp |
| Awesome Highlighter | http://www.awesomehighlighter.com/ |
| Vozme | http://vozme.com/index.php?lang=en |
| Clip Speak | http://clipspeak.codeplex.com |
| ReadPlease | http://www.readplease.com/ |
| Read & Write Gold | http://www.texthelp.com/North-America/our-products/readwrite |
| Kurzweil | http://www.kurzweiledu.com/default.html |

## Digital Textbooks (a sample listing)

| k-12 Flexbooks | http://www.ck12.org/flexbook/ |
|---|---|
| Pearson | http://www.pearsonschool.com |
| Textbook Publishers | http://www.eduplace.com/eservices/previews/index.jsp?state=oh |
| Apple Textbooks | http://www.apple.com/education/ibooks-textbooks/ |

## Literature and Trade Book Sites

| Gutenberg | http://www.gutenberg.org |
|---|---|
| OverDrive | http://www.overdrive.com |
| Book Share | www.bookshare.org |
| CISAM | http://cisam.ossb.oh.gov/ |
| NIMAC | http://www.nimac.us/ |
| Just Free Books | http://www.justfreebooks.info/ |
| Wired For Books | http://www.wiredforbooks.org/index2.htm |
| Old Time Radio | http://otr.net/ |
| Knowing Poe | http://knowingpoe.thinkport.org/default_flash.asp |
| Weekly Reader | www.weeklyreader.com |
| Librivox | http://librivox.org/ |
| Internet Archive | http://www.archive.org/details/texts |
| Open Library | http://openlibrary.org |
| AbleNet Weekly Reader Editions | http://www.ablenetinc.com/ |

*Site viability cannot be guaranteed as technology references change quickly.*

## Other resources: (adapted from OCALI)*

| | |
|---|---|
| **Developing Reading Skills**<br><br>**Goodwill Community Foundation: Reading Activities**<br><br>Designed for older students or adults learning to read.<br><br>Learn and practice reading the top 1,000 most frequently used words | http://www.gcflearnfree.org/reading |
| **Read Write Think** | http://www.readwritethink.org/parent-afterschool-resources/ |
| **Barnes & Noble Lexile Reading Level Wizard**<br><br>Find books by reading level | http://www.barnesandnoble.com/reading-level-reading-books-lexile/search.asp?cds2Pid=30223 |
| **Read Print**<br><br>A free online book library of classic Literature (over 8,000 titles). Text only. | http://www.readprint.com/ |
| **60 second Recap**<br><br>Irresistible to today's teens.<br><br>60 second Recap video albums cover the overview, plot, characters, context, motifs and the conclusion of a literature classic. | http://www.60secondrecap.com/ |

Also NOTE:

Apple's Special Education App Store:

http://www.apple.com/education/special-education/

*Readers should be aware that Internet websites offered as citations and/or sources for further information may have changed or disappeared between the time this book was written and when it is read.*

# Note Taking

It might seem logical that the actual taking of notes is not what's important, but rather the information that the notes contain. Nevertheless, when students take notes there is a level of engagement with the material that facilitates learning.

Here are some quick tips to help with note taking:

> Write notes in legible block printing. Some students cannot read and process cursive handwriting. It's also important to remember that ALL CAPS are very hard to read because the letters are closer together, and there is less space between the words as well.

> Some students have difficulty with "far point copying." These students take notes letter by letter instead of hearing, remembering and recording phrases. Make a set of notes available to these students either online, or through a peer scribe or classroom notebook.

> Other students cannot multitask, so it is difficult or impossible for them to take notes and listen at the same time. If they are copying information, they cannot simultaneously reflect, learn or otherwise engage with the material. The simple solution is to provide these students with a highlighter and a complete copy of the notes at the beginning of class. Underline key words or phrases and ask the student to highlight those items on their copy of the lecture. In another example, if you give a student a copy of a PowerPoint, have the student work with a partner to go back and paraphrase each slide after every three presented slides.

> Other students with special needs have a disability with far point copying, which means they cannot process information posted at a distance longer than their arm. A common modification for these students is to have someone else take notes for them. However, it is not a good use of resources to have an adult sit in class and take notes for a student. See scribe options on the next few pages.

**Fill-in-the-Blank or Skeleton Notes:**

Below is an example of fill-in-the-blank notes, which will allow some students with disabilities to benefit from the learning opportunity that note taking offers. Students are provided with some of the key information and a structure to follow. The check mark in the review bar denotes how many times the student has studied the notes in class (see page 28 for the importance of repetition when committing material to memory).

---

Chapter 20    Cell Reproduction

I. All life starts out as _____ _____.

    A.

    B.

II. _____ _____ are formed

    by _____ _____.

III. Types of Cell Division

    A. Mitosis: Definition

        1. Mitosis is used for replacement of:

            a.

            b.

            c.

            d.

            e.

---

Maze notes version: use fill-in-the-blank notes, but provide students with a word bank to choose from in parentheses near the appropriate blank. For students with far point copying and spelling issues, it helps them fill in the blanks correctly. Example:

The three important aspects of WWII

_____(socialize, social, emotional)

_____(politics, elections, political)

_____(economic, economy, ecology)

## Note Taking Accommodations

At the University level, students with disabilities may qualify to receive accommodations under Section 504 of the law. One common accommodation is to have a classroom note-taker, which often entails assigning a student to the task. Both carbon paper and NCR (no carbon required) paper are available at local business supply stores. These low-technology items allow students to receive instant copies of peer notes in a classroom. Higher technology options might include a student taking notes on a hardware device (laptop, tablet, electronic blackboard) and emailing or "bumping" the notes to their friends. Another option is for the teacher to post notes on a website. Students can either download them before class or print them off of the electronic blackboard.

**SPECIAL STRATEGY**

### The Model Classroom Notebook

Ask a few students to volunteer to keep a sample classroom notebook. Every time a teacher gives out notes or handouts, the volunteers add the information to the model classroom notebook. Imagine having a three-ring binder with tabbed divider sections, organized with a copy of everything from classroom handouts, a list of homework assignments, copies of quizzes, etc. Students who need to organize their notebooks, are missing a copy of the notes, or were absent from class, can sign out the model notebook and use it as an exemplar sample to update and organize their own information. Special education teachers, ELL teachers, and other specialists can instantly access information a child might need for your classroom.

This notice was posted on the bulletin board at a local university.

# CALL TODAY

# NOTE TAKERS NEEDED

## SPRING SEMESTER

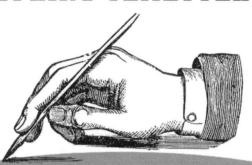

*The Disability Resource Office needs people to take notes in class for students with disabilities.*

Interested students must:

- Have a minimum GPA of 3.0
- Be able to take clear, well-written notes
- Attend each class
- Enjoy working with peers

Compensation is **$7.50** per hour

For more information, please come into the DRO, Engleman 23, or call us at **392-6828**.

# Note Taking Accommodations
## A list of popular ideas

➢ Use a graphic organizer

➢ Provide a copy of teacher's notes

➢ Provide a copy of the lesson online

➢ Skeleton or maze outline

➢ Carbon or NCR notes from a peer

➢ Note taking notebook in the classroom

➢ When writing notes on the board, highlight or underline key words or phases

➢ Three column notes (include the memory device, see page 114)

➢ Print notes - for some students, cursive is difficult to read

➢ Use a reveal method to show only one or two lines at a time (cover up information not being discussed to help the student focus)

➢ Print notes from a Power Point presentation (two slides per pages)

➢ Sketch notes

➢ Teach to multiple intelligences and learning styles

## Carbon notes

If you have a good note taker in your classroom, you can provide that student with a piece of carbon paper or some NCR (no carbon required) paper. This can be invaluable not only for those students who have difficulty taking notes, but also for students that were out sick, as well as for students who missed a few points. Special educators will also find the collection of notes helpful when creating pre-teaching modules and study guides.

## Notebook partners

When you're switching gears between lessons, a quick sponge activity is to have students pair up and check each other's notebooks. Many students lack organizational skills, and it helps them keep on track before material is lost. Good notes are the best kind of study guide. Tip: Provide students with a list or checklist of the items they should have in their notebooks.

**Classroom assignment notebook**

In addition to the collection of notes at the back of the classroom, it can be helpful to collect the assignments in a notebook as well. One student may be assigned to keep it current. It helps foster independence for students who were absent or missed writing down the assignment.

**Three-column notes**

Many teachers subscribe to two-column or Cornell notes, which consist of a narrow left-hand column for keywords and a broader right-hand column for note taking. In three-column notes, the third column contains a strategy for unlocking the content. In the first example below, the key word "mitosis" is written in the first column, it is defined in the second, and the third column contains a memory device, much like the linking strategy discussed on pages 23-26.

The second example shows a question/prediction strategy. The question or prediction is placed in column one. At the end of the section, the student writes down the answer to the prediction and the reference page where that answer was found.

Example 1: Types of Cell Division

| Key words | Definitions | Memory Device |
|---|---|---|
| Mitosis | • cell division<br>• two new daughter cells | My toes itch (two new toes grew on my feet and they itch). |

Example 2: *White Fang* by Jack London

| Question / Prediction | Answer | Page number |
|---|---|---|
| P: White Fang and Kiche will escape. | Kiche was taken away by other Tribesmen. White Fang waited until nightfall and ran away. | p. 127 |

**Sketch notes**

Sketch notes are particularly effective at helping students retain content details from the middle of the lesson, the portion that is always more difficult to remember. You might have students take regular notes up to the point where you need them to recall specific details. To facilitate sketch notes, have students take a blank sheet of paper and fold it in half three times so that the crease lines forms eight boxes, then number the boxes 1 through 8 (see page 117).

Read a section of information. When you come to a memorable detail, ask the students to draw a sketch in box 1. Continue the process for as many boxes as you need. Some students may want to write some key words with their sketches, and that's fine.

This strategy works particularly well in social studies or science, where the topic is often a series of events that link together. You will find that it is a real memory booster, and it also levels the playing field: students who are more artistic rather than verbal or auditory will have an opportunity to take notes. It's also fun, and it works really well in a secondary classroom.

**TEACHING TIP**

### Differentiate with Sketch Notes

Example 1:  After students have completed their sketch notes, you can use the notes for a variety of learning activities. For example: have the students erase/remove the numbers from their boxes and then, using scissors, cut their notes up into boxes. Students place the cut up note boxes in an envelope and give them to their learning partner.  The learning partner has to assemble the notes in the proper order and defend or justify why the notes should be in that order.

Example 2: Students could also use the boxes to play a memory game.  The students form teams of three. Each team member shuffles their boxes and places them so the blank side is up, and the sketched side is face down. One student at a time turns a box over and has to explain how the information fits into the day's lesson. Teams alternate. The "sketcher" decides if the "player's" description was accurate and explains why or why not.

Following is a classroom example of how you might use sketch notes.

# Sketch Notes
## The Statue of Liberty

1.  The statue of liberty was erected in 1886. It was a gift from the people of France to the people of the United States to celebrate U.S. independence and French-American friendship. It was the idea of French politician Edouard Rene de Laboulaye in 1870. It was designed by French sculptor Frederic Bartholdi. The engineer for the statue was Alexandre-Gustave Eiffel, who built the Eiffel tower.

2.  The statue depicts Liberty holding a torch, which represents progress and enlightenment. Liberty wears a crown with seven spikes that look like the sun's rays. The number seven represented the seven seas and the seven continents. The sculptor used his mother's face as the model for Liberty's face.

3.  Laboulaye raised the money to build the statue. Donations came from all levels of French society, including ordinary citizens and school children.

4.  The U.S. built the pedestal and foundation. As in France, the funds came from ordinary people, such as schoolchildren, office workers and elderly people, who donated what they could. A total of $102,000 was raised from 120,000 people. 80% of the contributions were less than one dollar.

5.  The statue was brought to America on board a ship called the Isere. 200,000 people lined the docks and hundreds of boats put to sea to welcome the Isere as it came into New York harbor.

6.  Laboulaye had died in 1883. The new chairman of the French committee was Ferdinand de Lesseps. U.S. President Grover Cleveland presided over the dedication. No members of the general public were admitted on the island for the ceremony – only dignitaries. There were only two women present: Bertholdi's wife and de Lessep's granddaughter. Women were denied the right to be present because the men claimed the women might be trampled in the crowd. Suffragists, who were trying to win the right to vote and other rights for women, were offended. They chartered a boat and got as close as they could to the island in order to watch the ceremony from the water.

7.  On the morning of the dedication, there was a parade consisting of marching bands from all across America. As many as one million people attended. As the parade passed the New York Stock Exchange, stock traders threw ticker tape from the windows, which started the tradition of ticker tape parades.

8.  Emma Lazarus, a Jewish American woman and a member of the suffragist movement, wrote a poem called The New Colossus, which is written out on a bronze plaque at the base of the statue. It contains the famous lines: "Give me your tired, your poor, your huddled masses yearning to breathe free."

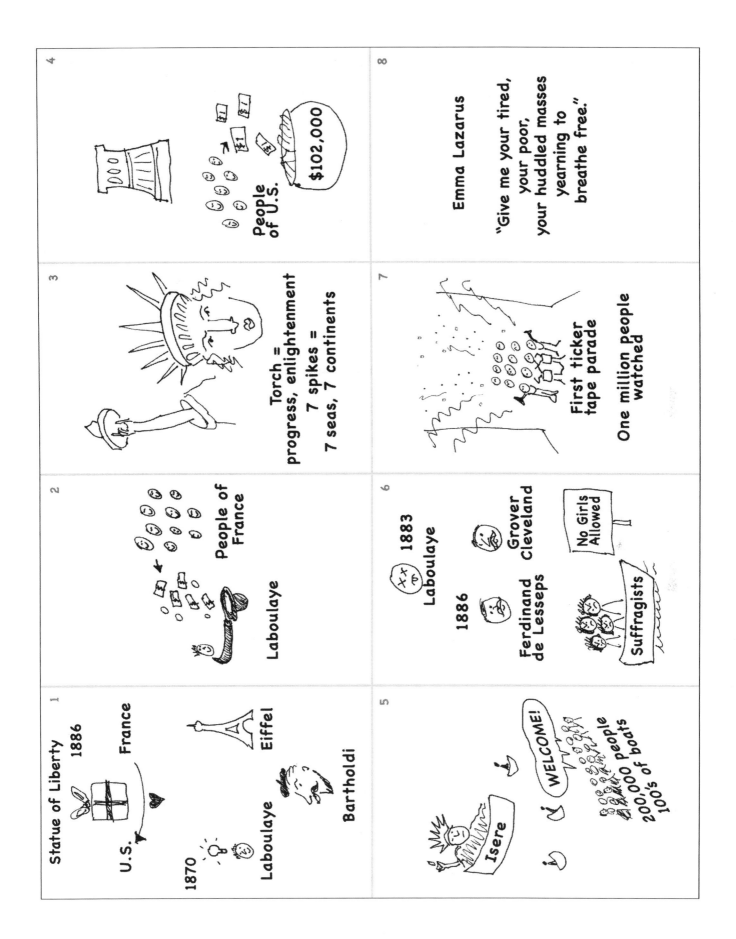

# Accommodating Classwork

Here is an example of a Type 1 accommodation. Students were asked to read a selection in their social studies textbook and then answer the corresponding questions. To accommodate this task for a student with reading and writing issues, the teacher created a targeted reading list. The student read only the assigned paragraphs and then used the "RAP" strategy to paraphrase them.

The RAP strategy consists of: **R**eading text silently; **A**sking yourself what it was about (the main idea); **P**utting the main idea and details into your own words.

In the example below, when the student reads the assigned paragraph on page 112 in section A, the paraphrasing of that selection should answer question #1 on the worksheet.

Question 1
pg 112, Section A, Paragraph 1

Question 2:
pg 113, Section B, Paragraph 1

Question 3:
pg 113, Section B, Paragraph 2

Question 4:
pg 113, Section B, Paragraph 3

Question 5:
pg 113, Section C, Paragraph 1

Question 6:
pg 114, Section C, Paragraph 3

Question 7:
pg 114, Section D, Paragraph 3

Question 8:
pg 114, Section D, Paragraph 5

Question 9:
pg 114, Section D, Paragraph 5, Sentence 5

Question 10:
pg 115, Section E, Paragraph 2

# Modifying for Auditory Processing

Students with an auditory processing disorder have difficulty recognizing and interpreting sounds, especially the spoken word. Here is a list of strategies to help students hear in the classroom:

## Tips to help improve students' listening skills

- ❖ Begin with key phrases:
  - ➢ "The topic is…"
  - ➢ "Let me repeat this… you will see it again…I will wait while you copy this down"
  - ➢ "This is a test question…"
  - ➢ "Directions!"
- ❖ Put a "menu of the day" on the board outlining the lesson tasks (see page 121).
- ❖ Teach students how to listen in your classroom: "Here is what listening looks and sounds like to me." "This is what I expect to see and hear you do when I call 'Listen up.'"
- ❖ Work with students individually to create a private/discreet signal (like tugging your ear) to help redirect them when they veer off-task.
- ❖ See some lesson plans for teaching listening skills on page 122.

## Tips for giving directions

- ❖ Get the students' full attention before you begin:
  - ➢ Flick the lights
  - ➢ Use a hand signal
  - ➢ Close the door
  - ➢ Count back from 3: "3…2…1…"
- ❖ Use a different tone:
  - ➢ Whisper an answer to a test question
  - ➢ Get very excited

❖ Use visuals and paired activities to give directions:

> ➤ Give directions in no more than three steps at a time

> ➤ Use fingers to indicate step 1, step 2...

> ➤ Teach students to summarize or paraphrase key points in pairs

> ➤ Turn to your neighbor activity: "Give me a minute" (see below)

**SPECIAL STRATEGY**

**Give Me A Minute**

In pairs, students are given one minute to summarize all of the tasks/procedures that must be accomplished over the class period.

An occasional strategy is to have a student repeat the directions after you say them. If you have a student who never pays attention, designate him as the class Direction Repeater. Then tell the class, "If anybody has any questions on the directions, you can see Paul over here." This strategy works if there are a few kids that go over and ask Paul, who repeats the directions a couple of times. Then everybody can get to work, and by the time he settles down to work, Paul has heard the directions at least three times. However, I once had a situation where everybody in the classroom had to visit with Paul and ask him directions; there were kids lined up around the corner. In that case, we had to drop that strategy, but you might find it works once in awhile until they catch on.

When you're giving directions, a simple way to chunk directions without rewriting them is to outline the first, second and third steps, accompanied by simple hand gestures.

> ➤ First, we're going to --

> ➤ The second thing I ask you to do is --

> ➤ And then the third part is --

# Menu of the Day

Have you ever been in a car with children who ask, "Are we there yet?"

To avoid the classroom version of the "Are we there yet?" syndrome, we can post a Menu of the Day, which curtails impatience by allowing students to monitor progress through the curriculum.

---

### Menu of the Day

- Review and collect last night's homework

- Write down tonight's homework

- Identify Lesson objective

- Take sideline notes on the civil war

- Group work: Complete the "Compare and Contrast" chart

- Exit Ticket: What were three causes of the civil war?

---

## SPECIAL STRATEGY

### For Restless Students

If you have students that like to get up and move, invite them to come up to the board and "cross the item off the list" after it is completed. This helps create a sense of accomplishment and allows them a mini kinesthetic break.

# Example Lesson Plans
## Listening Skills

Listening is something that we expect students to do constantly although they may never have learned the skill. One approach is to return to the basics: what does listening look and sound like?

| | | T chart | |
|---|---|---|---|
| | | looks like | sounds like |

**Objective:**
- To learn good listening behaviors

**Materials:**
- T chart of what good listening looks like and sounds like
- Markers

**Previous lesson:**
- Students learned the 5 listening techniques

**Method:**
- Students brainstorm in groups – what good listeners look like and sound like
- T-charts are shared with the class
- Students role-play good listening and poor listening in groups and pairs.

**Variation:**
- Students role-play a teacher and other students showing good and poor listening skills. Students journal about their feelings and the effect of good listening in the classroom and with peers.

---

**Objective**
- Infuse listening skills into the curriculum

**Materials:**
- Topics on slips of paper covered in current unit

**Review:**
- Review listening strategies

**Previous Lesson:**
- Yesterday students role-played each listening strategy

**Method:**
- Pairs of students face each other
- Pairs determine sender and receiver roles
- Sender pulls a slip from a jar. The slip has a topic covered in a recent lesson. The sender spends one minute telling the receiver everything he/she knows about the topic. The receiver then practices a specified good listening technique (i.e. clarifying).

**Variations:**
1. Each person takes turns covering a different topic as a sender.
2. The receiver practices, summarizing at the end of one minute.
3. Form groups of three, allowing for one observer. The observer monitors body language and attending behaviors.

| | |
|---|---|
| Objective | • To discuss the role of attitude in the classroom |
| Material: | • Journals |
| Previous Lesson: | • |
| Method: | • Teacher brainstorms with students: synonyms for the word "attitude" |

• Teacher give the class the following scenario:

> "Two workers are up for a big promotion. Only one of them will get the promotion, which includes a big raise and a company car. The workers are evenly qualified in ability to do the job; however, one worker has a good attitude and one worker has a poor attitude while at work. ..."

• Teacher and students decide what the "good" and the "poor" attitude students look like on this job

• The teacher asks, "Who should get the promotion?"

• Students work in cooperative groups and create a chart outlining who should and shouldn't get the promotion and why they made their decision.

• Have each group present their "case" to the class (a.k.a. The Promotion Panel). Have each group give three reasons why their candidate is the best choice.

• Next give the students a hypothetical scenario from your school. The two students have borderline grades. One student has a poor attitude in the classroom and one student has a good attitude in the classroom. How should the teacher grade the students? Have students react in a journal assignment for homework.

| | |
|---|---|
| Follow up: | • Have students share journals |
| | • How does attitude influence success? |

# Strategies for Teaching Vocabulary

**Flash cards**
(traditional 3 x 5 card with the word on front and the definition on back)

> ➢ Electronic internet sources: (sampling)
>
> http://www.proprofs.com/flashcards/
>
> http://www.flashcardmachine.com/
>
> http://www.scholastic.com/kids/homework/flashcards.htm

> ➢ Apps: (sampling)
>
> http://itunes.apple.com/us/app/flashcards-deluxe/id307840670?mt=8
>
> http://www.droidforums.net/forum/droid-applications/5536-review-flashcard-apps-droid.html

**Flash cards with memory devices**
(pictures, words, stories)

**Use Name Badge-Sized Labels to Create Flash Cards**

Stick adhesive-backed name badge labels onto 3 x 5 cards. These labels also fit PERFECTLY on playing cards. Cover the cards with labels, placing the vocabulary word on one side and the definition on the other.

**Vocabulary strips**
(cut a page of vocabulary words into strips)

| Vocabulary word | Definition |
|---|---|
| Vocabulary word | Definition |

## Vocabulary word cards
(create these using label maker tools in a word processor program)

FRONT

| Vocabulary word | Vocabulary word |
|---|---|
| Vocabulary word | Vocabulary word |

BACK

| Definition | Definition |
|---|---|
| Definition | Definition |

## Vocabulary File Box
Alphabetize a collection of 3 x 5 cards, each with a vocabulary word and its definition. Store the cards in a recipe file box for student access. For other disciplines such as math or science, the cards can be used to outline a process.

## Flip book (words or pictures)

**SPECIAL STRATEGY**

### A Simple Flip Book for the Secondary Classroom

Take four different colored pieces of paper and lay them out vertically so that they are fanned out (showing about two inches of each color). Fold the stack in half and place two staples at the top of the crease. Students can use this flip book to write vocabulary words or to create study guides.

## Venn Diagrams
These are used to demonstrate the relationships between different groups of things. One visual way to make an impact with Venn Diagrams is to cut circles out of transparent plastic folders from two different colors. Overlap the two circles. Where the two colors intersect, a third color is created to show areas of similarity. (Example: a yellow circle intersects a blue circle and creates an overlap area of green.)

Another fun way to use Venn diagrams is through the use of hula hoops propped up against the wall. Give the students sticky notes and divide them into two groups. One side lists all the characteristics of one group of things, the other side lists the characteristics of another. Then the groups take turns taking the sticky notes that list common characteristics and move them to the area where the hula hoops intersect (see below). This activity introduces kinesthetics into the classroom. Because of the visuals, it helps alleviate inattention.

Venn diagrams can also be created on the classroom electronic projection boards and tablets. Students enjoy manipulating and moving objects around as they are allowed to kinesthetically participate in the lesson.

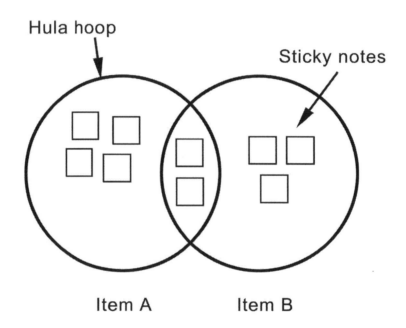

# Modify Content Using Low-Tech Materials

## White boards

Lap-sized white boards are an effective way to keep students engaged with content, and they're perfect for quick reviews: have the students write down the answer to a question with dry erase markers and then display their answers by holding up the boards.

An inexpensive solution to purchasing commercial white boards is to buy a large piece of shower board from a home construction supply store. Generally, the staff will cut the board to size for free if you tell them you're a teacher. You can get about 35 lap sized white boards from one piece of shower board.

I often cut white boards into small strips (about 3" x 12"). I use these strips in the classroom for quick activities to promote whole classroom responses. For example, I have students write "agree" on one end of the board and "disagree" on the other end. Then I ask general questions and students vote by holding up their answer.

See the "Pass the Problem" activity on page 163.

### SPECIAL STRATEGY

### Help for Students with Grapho-Motor Issues

Some students have difficulty writing on a plain white board. To address this issue, there are dry erase boards available that have raised lines. You can find them at: www.dryerase.com

For math, try white boards with primary tablet writing lines. Hold the white board vertically so the lines create columns. The columns keep numbers aligned for calculations, such as adding decimals.

**Restickable Surface**

Spray a restickable adhesive (such as 3M™ Spray Mount Adhesive) on a non-tactile surface plastic tablecloth. Hang the tablecloth on the wall. Chart paper, 3 x 5 cards and student work will all adhere to the tablecloth and can be removed when you are done. This low-tack adhesive allows you to rearrange items without removing the paint from classroom walls. You can organize students into small groups for a bit of kinesthetic activity such as:

- ➤ Brainstorming
- ➤ Categorizing
- ➤ Arranging
- ➤ Compare/Contrast
- ➤ Problem solving

### SPECIAL STRATEGY

**Sequencing Activities Using Restickable Spray Mount Adhesive**

Spray a smooth plastic tablecloth (like the inexpensive ones at the dollar store) with the spray mount to create a sticky surface.

Take a series of math problems and write them on strips of paper (one strip per step). Shuffle the papers for each problem and put one complete problem in an envelope. Have students work in pairs to organize the strips of paper into the proper order by sticking the strips to the table cloth to solve each of the equations. Then have students "justify" or "argue" why the sequence is correct.

Another idea:

Take a PowerPoint from a lecture and cut the slides into separate boxes. Shuffle the slides. Have the students organize the PowerPoint slides back into the proper order by sticking them on the table cloth. Then have students orally summarize the key points of the lecture from their determined order.

# The Great Homework Debate: Can't versus Won't

Before we focus on the completion of the homework by a student with a disability, we must first "test" the homework to ensure the student is:

1. Capable of completing the homework independently
    a. The homework is provided on the student's INDEPENDENT reading level
    b. The student is given alternative ways of writing or recording the homework
    c. The homework is a reflection of practice and not a test of new learning
    d. The homework is NOT at cross purposes with the IEP.

2. The second test is, "Does the homework allow for the student to practice in the appropriate amount of time?"
    a. Can the student complete three examples instead of five to demonstrate competency in the materials?
    b. Can the student demonstrate competency in an alternative format?
    c. Does the homework require the student to "teach themselves." If so, is this what additional resources will be provided for the student to have a second "reteaching" of the material (i.e. a lecture that is taped.)
    d. How will you account for the extra time that it takes the learner with the biggest academic discrepancy to complete the same tasks as others? Where will the extra time come from?

Once you are sure:
1. The student has appropriate homework
2. It is appropriate to give the student homework

Then it may be time to modify the homework further, in order for the student to have equal access and equal opportunity in the classroom.

When students do not turn in homework, it is important to determine why the student isn't doing the assignment. In some cases, homework may require modifications in order to ensure student success and learning.

If a student CAN'T do the work, here are a few ideas*:

  ➢ Provide the student with an outline of the work
  ➢ Have students complete an outline of key ideas instead of answering questions
  ➢ Provide books on tape
  ➢ Show students how to access online outlines of the materials or provide them to the students
  ➢ Supply a copy of abridged copies of the reading
  ➢ Use films and videos that augment learning

- ➢ Use motivational material
- ➢ Give alternative assignments with the same theme
- ➢ Assign the student a highlighted book with answers pre-highlighted *
- ➢ Have the student attend a homework club after school
- ➢ Homework help line with calling hours
- ➢ Homework lab in school
- ➢ Help the student set up a study calendar with a study schedule
- ➢ Don't assign it
- ➢ Weight their grades more on a project in their area of intelligence (multiple intelligence theory) than homework
- ➢ Call parents when three homework assignments have been missed or poorly done
- ➢ Conduct team conference after five missed or poorly done homework assignments
- ➢ Assign a homework buddy (someone they can do their homework with, or perhaps accept homework from one of the students to count for both of them)

How do you know students WON'T do their homework? While we certainly have students that refuse to complete work, it is possible that there are other factors that impede a student from completing homework. If a student WON'T do the work, here are a few ideas**:

- ➢ Create a homework contract with the student
- ➢ Initiate a parent conference
- ➢ Make sure it is not a "can't"
- ➢ Give choices, such as providing homework "Tic-tac-toe"
- ➢ Spend time with the student and do the work together
- ➢ Fax or email parents the homework
- ➢ Post the homework on a blog or on voicemail
- ➢ Sign the homework log on a daily basis
- ➢ Do it in class
- ➢ Peer tutor from the same class/homework buddy

\* In some cases, these can be purchased online. Search "used textbooks." The inexpensive ones with highlighting and notes in them are the ones you want!

\*\* Be sure and document how you were able to determine "can't versus won't" if a student with an IEP fails a class because of homework. You should have documentation that shows how you were able to determine "can't versus won't" and what steps you took to rectify the situation. For example: if a student reads on a 4th grade reading level and the homework is generated from the 9th grade level textbook, is it reasonable that the student be held accountable for work he or she cannot read independently? Should there be a failing grade for homework when the material was beyond the student's reading ability?

# General Education Strategy List

In pursuit of our goal to teach every student, we sometimes realize that a student needs some extra help, even if there is no identified learning disability. Accommodations and modifications are not just for students with IEPs - they also work well for students with at-risk needs. The law does not say we can only accommodate if a student has an IEP on file; we can in fact try to meet the needs of any student through the use of modifications and accommodations.

However, without an IEP, modifications that helped the student learn might not be passed along to subsequent teachers. One thing teachers can do is to list strategies that worked for a particular student and give them to the principal or to a guidance counselor who can pass the information on to the next year's teacher. That way, teachers know that a particular student has received some sort of modification or an accommodation, and they don't have to reinvent the wheel as they try to determine the best strategy to help the student master the content. This type of documentation can be particularly helpful at the secondary school level where, from one grade to the next, there aren't necessarily opportunities to confer on individual cases. Such conferences are a little easier at the elementary school level.

On pages 133 and 134, there is a General Education Strategy List that was developed for the high school level. This strategy sheet gets filed in the cume file because it is not a special education document. However, if you choose to use this form, it would be wise to discuss it with the student's parent and say, "Your child is struggling in my class and needs a little something extra. I'm going to do a few accommodations or modifications and keep track of them on this paper, which will then be placed in the child's file. That way, next year's teacher will have a resource if they need to find out what strategies worked for your child."

There is an accountability issue regarding whether teachers are doing what's right for students, and this is how we document it.

# Directions for the General Education Strategy List

This form is intended for regular education teachers to use for <u>any</u> student, on any level in their classroom who does not have a current I.E.P. on file.

1. Every student is entitled to a report card. Please fill out the child's report card based on <u>his/her</u> level of learning.

2. If you have made extensive modifications for a child, use the strategy checklist to indicate the type of modifications you use to provide the child with an appropriate education.

3. Please call or meet with the parent to explain the type of modifications you are—or will be—using.

4. If requested, send the parent a copy of the checklist at the end of the year (some parents may ask for them quarterly or twice a year).

5. Give the principal a copy to be filed in the cumulative file at the end of the school year.

6. PLEASE do not write "modified" on the student's report card. Modified is indicated on the strategy list.

7. The principal can devise a system for communicating which students can have a strategies list on file, and how to share that information from one year's teacher to the next. (For example, store the information on a list that is kept by the school guidance counselors.)

# General Education Strategy List

Student's  Name  _____

Teacher's  names  _____

_____

_____

_____

_____

School year _____ Grade _____

Previous Interventions

Date(s) and types (i.e. telephone, letter conference, progress report..) or parent contracts:

_____

_____

_____

Items discussed:

_____

_____

_____

_____

_____

_____

Please identify accommodations and strategies used for this child. Provide any needed explanations on the back of this form.

## Strategies for Content and Instructional Style

___ Multi-level curriculum
___ Curriculum Compacting

Differentiated Curriculum
Differentiated by:
___ Process
___ Product
___ Content

___ Alternate curriculum

___ Plan for learning style
___ Videotape student
___ Give directions: verbally, visually, model, by a peer
___ Have student teach to class
___ Daily assignment notebook, signed by parent/teacher
___ Allow student to redo, correct work for better grade
___ Alternate homework assignments
___ Step by step cards
___ Projects with steps and due dates for each step written down

___ Projects in lieu of tests
___ Special attention signal/cue
___ Special seating
___ Opportunities for movement (work, break/work, errand…)
___ Student writes on board surface
___ Verbal rehearsal
___ Cue cards
___ Use Multiple Intelligence Strength
   Specify area _____

## Strategies for Materials

___ Audio books
___ Provide visuals (transparency, graphic organizer)
___ Manipulatives for _____
___ Use of technology. Specify: _____
___ Use of calculator
___ Color code
___ Enhancement activities
___ Sticky notes
___ Extra set of books for home
___ Schedule taped to books or on wall
___ Mnemonics
___ Transparencies to write on
___ Special paper
___ Pencil/pen grips
___ Highlighter tools
___ Handheld white boards

## Strategies for Assistance

___ Use another adult (professional, volunteer, paraprofessional)
___ Peer tutor
___ Study buddy
___ Parent
___ Tutors other students in a lower grade or class level
___ Electronic recording device in school or at home
___ Computer program to reinforce concepts
___ Provide a copy of teacher's notes or online resources to support reading materials
   Specify: _____
___ Carbon Paper
___ Video
___ Outlined study notes

## Strategies for Assistance Continued

___ Guided outline
___ After school help
___ Community resources
___ Modeling
___ Consultants used _____ (title)

## Strategies for Evaluation

___ Challenge, Bonus questions on test
___ Extra project in lieu of test
___ Not counting portion of test in _____
___ Oral testing
___ Testing with directions on a tape recorder
___ Break test into sections
___ Untimed
___ Correct for a better grade
___ Portfolio assessment
___ No penalty for spelling errors
___ Reformatted test
___ Grades based on level of child's ability
___ Alternative grading
___ Alternate Assessment
___ Contract Grades

## Strategies for Positive Behavior Management

___ Special Attention Signal
___ Warning Signal
___ Behavior Management Plan (attach sample)
___ Responds to precision commands
___ Responds well to positive reinforcement
___ Contract (attach sample)
___ Token System
___ Sign in/out sheet
___ Chart Behavior Weekly
___ Proximity Control
___ Planned Ignoring
___ Mystery Motivator
___ Special seating _____
___ Weekly monitoring (phone or paper)
___ Warning Signal
___ Use of special reward

Other Comments:

_____
_____
_____
_____
_____
_____
_____
_____
_____
_____
_____
_____
_____
_____
_____
_____

**To be given to building principal for filing in the cumulative folder at the end of the school year.**

Signed:_____
_____
_____
_____
_____
_____
_____

cc: _____

_____

# Writing IEP Goals Based on Content Standards

Since 1997, the IDEA has mandated that IEP goals and objectives must be based on performance standards. Here is an example of a performance standard and how you might write a goal for students needing Type 1 through Type 4 accommodations and modifications.

Currently, under the Common Core State Standards (CCSS), the following is articulated for students with disabilities: (copied and pasted into the text left from this website:

http://www.corestandards.org/assets/application-to-students-with-disabilities.pdf

Students with disabilities are a heterogeneous group with one common characteristic: the presence of disabling conditions that significantly hinder their abilities to benefit from general education (IDEA 34 CFR §300.39, 2004). Therefore, *how* these high standards are taught and assessed is of the utmost importance in reaching this diverse group of students. In order for students with disabilities to meet high academic standards and to fully demonstrate their conceptual and procedural knowledge and skills in mathematics, reading, writing, speaking and listening (English language arts), their instruction must incorporate supports and accommodations, including:

➢ Supports and related services designed to meet the unique needs of these students and to enable their access to the general education curriculum (IDEA 34 CFR §300.34, 2004).

➢ An Individualized Education Program (IEP)1 which includes annual goals aligned with and chosen to facilitate their attainment of grade-level academic standards.

➢ Teachers and specialized instructional support personnel who are prepared and qualified to deliver high-quality, evidence-based, individualized instruction and support services.

## Performance Standard

Cite strong and thorough textual evidence to support analysis of what the text says explicitly, as well as inferences drawn from the text. (Example: CCSS – GR 9-10, Reading Standards for Literature, Key Information and Details, 1.)

Sample IEP goal based on the CCSS and student needs (data).

Given a reading passage of fewer than 150 words on the student's grade level, the student will orally express to a peer or into a recorder a plausible theme the central theme of a reading, or an inference about the text, and ask three HOT (higher order thinking) questions, as measured by an inference checklist in seven out of eight trials.

# Universal Objectives for Career Clusters

The Connecticut 'School to Career' project lists career clusters that encompass every conceivable job in the world.

http://www.sde.ct.gov/sde/lib/sde/PDF/DEPS/Career/WB/mentoring.pdf

Each cluster has a list of employability traits, which I cross-referenced to obtain a list of objectives that were universal to all career clusters. This list can be very helpful for teachers engaged in writing individualized transition plans (ITPs) or other types of individual learning plans for students aged 14 and over. Assuming that a student will hold a job at some point, consider the following objectives for students with disabilities. Therefore, some of the child's goals, should consider this connection when incorporating goals for school and career readiness at the secondary level.

The student must learn to:

- Take initiative as a situation demands
- Assume responsibility for own actions
- Maintain high standards of personal behavior
- Follow verbal and written instructions
- Work without close supervision
- Work effectively under stress
- Accept personal responsibility for production/quality
- Keep personal conflicts from impeding performance
- Seek new challenges and maintain a professional image
- Respond constructively to constructive criticism

- Work effectively in a team
- Follow verbal and written instructions
- Provide support to others
- Foster creativity and innovation
- Communicate in a professional manner
- Accept changes without complaint
- Handle several projects or tasks simultaneously
- Transfer newly acquired knowledge and skills to new situations
- Adjust personal style according to the demands of the situation
- Recognize that an integral part of the job is the ability to perform different tasks during changeovers, breakdowns, and emergencies

"With students, parents and teachers all on the same page and working together for shared goals, we can ensure that students make progress each year and graduate from school prepared to succeed in college and in a modern workforce." (www.corestandards.org)

Travelers Insurance Company in Hartford, CT, published a list of employee skills in demand. In response to a question about why organizational skills were the number one priority, the author of the list, Peter Zakai, responded: "I can train someone to write a good memo for our company, but I have a harder time training employees about how to solve problems and organize."

If we can help students develop these basic skills, we are really giving them an advantage as they set out into the world looking for employment. Consider how some of these skills need to be incorporated into the IEP for school to career readiness. What is their connection to the common core state standards?

## The Skills Travelers Insurance Needs

- Organizational Skills
- Decision Making
- Writing
- Problem solving
- Interpersonal/Human Relations
- Learning/Using Software
- Knowledge of Company Products & Service
- Self-Confidence and Motivation
- Working in Teams
- Proofreading
- Speaking English Clearly and Correctly
- Reading Quickly/Comprehension
- Keyboarding
- Telephone Skills
- Basic Math
- Appropriate Work Behavior
- Basic Reading
- General Office Skills

## Accountability for the IEP

As defined by the National Education Association, general education teachers are responsible for all of the students in the classroom. However, best practice dictates that two teachers should work together in a collaborative manner when including a student with disabilities. The special education teacher and the general education teacher share responsibility for educating the student.*

As a special education teacher, I often found that my general education partners had difficulty maintaining all of the information in the IEP. They weren't sure who was in charge of that information or who was responsible for delivering the modification.

The IEP contains a great deal of information and often runs to many pages, so it can be an intimidating document. Providing my general education partners with the "IEP at a Glance" on page 139 allowed them to glean the essential information they needed to know about a student without having to go into excess detail. On page 140, there is a reproducible blank version for your convenience.

*For more information on who is accountable and/or responsible for IEP implementation, please see this website for case law: http://www.wrightslaw.com/caselaw.htm. Ultimately, teachers should review the IEP, taking special care to note who is listed as an implementer. If general education staff is listed, then the teachers involved with the student should collaborate to determine the mechanics of the implementation. Ultimately, it is not as important who does the implementation, but that the implementation is done in accordance with the IEP document.

Sample

# **IEP at a Glance**

Student Name: Jennifer Johnson — Grade 10

Case Manager: Sonya Kunkel

Disability Information: L.D. (primary) auditory processing deficit and A.D.D. (secondary).

Strengths/Best Learning Styles: Jen is a kinesthetic learner. She does well when she has an active job in the classroom. Visual depictions, graphs, and 3-D models support her learning. She is a talented artist.

Modifications: Skeleton notes, preferential seating in the back of the class (to allow for movement), sketch notes, extra time on dictated tests, allow her to get up and move (sharpen pencil, get a drink...etc.)

Comments: Call or email parents when she falls behind on more than 3 assignments

---------------------------------------------------------------------------------

Student Name: Lee Trang – Orange Team

Case Manager: Sonya Kunkel

Disability Information: L.D. – dyslexia, reading difficulties, reversals in reading and writing

Strengths/Best Learning Styles: An auditory learner, takes notes on his iPad, is willing to seek out extra help, works hard, comprehends best when books can be previewed on mp3 beforehand w/ pre-taught intro to vocabulary.

Modifications: Allow special access to computer lab for printing and use of Internet. Provide reading material in advance (to Special Education Dept.) Peer-partnered reading of in-class material tests reader (assignments made in advance).

Comments: Lee is very sensitive about his disability. He is a very responsible student and does not like to be singled out.

---------------------------------------------------------------------------------

*Computer-generated IEPs at a glance are often less detailed and more generic. Be sure relevant details (as in the above example) are included, and eliminate extraneous information.*

# IEP at a Glance

Student Name:

Case Manager:

Disability Information:

Strengths/Best Learning Styles:

Modifications:

Comments:

-----------------------------------------------------------------------------------

Student Name:

Case Manager:

Disability Information:

Strengths/Best Learning Styles:

Modifications:

Comments:

# The IEP According to Dr. Seuss

*Author unknown*

*Do you like these IEPs?*

    I do not like these IEPS

    I do not like them, Jeez Louise.

    We test, we check, we plan, we meet

    But nothing ever seems complete.

*Would you, could you, like the form?*

    I do not like the form I see; Not page 1, not 2, not 3.

    Another change, a brand new box

    I think we all have lost our rocks.

*Could you all meet here or there?*

    We could not all meet here or there. We cannot all fit anywhere.

    Not in a room, not in the hall, there seems to be no space at all.

*Would you, could you, meet again?*

    I cannot meet again next week; no lunch no prep, please hear me speak.

    No, not at dusk. No, not at dawn; at 4 pm I should be gone.

*Could you hear while all speak out? Would you write the words they spout?*

    I could not hear, I would not write, this does not need to be a fight.

    Sign here, date there, make this, check that,

    Beware the student's advocate.

*You do not like them, so you say.*

*Try again! and so you may.*

COLLABORATING
for INCLUSION

# Collaborative Models

For inclusion to happen effectively, some kind of collaborative model must be in place. At one end of the collaborative continuum, there is the consultation model; at the other end, there is co-teaching.

| External to the classroom | Internal to the classroom |
| --- | --- |

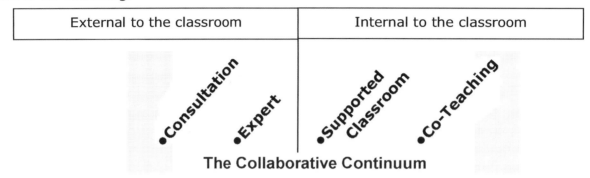

**The Collaborative Continuum**

## Consultation model

Planning time is vital if teachers are to provide each other necessary supports and services. When I was a special education teacher, I quickly learned that I would never be able to meet with all of the other teachers on my list if my plan period was at the same time every day. The solution to this problem was to stagger the time slot for my plan period. With a consultation-type schedule, I was available to consult with all of the other teachers at some point throughout the week.

In the consultation model, teachers meet as often as necessary - once a week, or once every two or three weeks - to review modifications and discuss students' progress. The special education teacher provides direct support to the general education teacher and indirect support to students.

## Expert model

In this model, the special education teacher is available to consult on an as-needed basis. The expert model is effective when including a small number of students with disabilities, but it does not work very well for a large number of students.

## Supported classroom model

This model does not require planning. In a supported classroom, a <u>paraprofessional</u> drifts around the classroom, offering assistance as needed. A special education teacher might offer itinerant support for general education teachers who have a specific need for two professionals in the classroom, such as a lab or test. It is sometimes necessary, but it isn't a model that is used on a consistent basis by a professional.

## Co-Teaching model

In this model, a special education teacher and a general education teacher enter into a contract that they will teach professionally together simultaneously.

# Supporting Inclusion through Collaborative Programming

## Collaborative meetings

Teachers meet at regularly scheduled intervals to proactively plan for success at the students' point of instruction (not supported after the fact.) Meetings should be set in stone BEFORE student schedules are made. It is the HIGHEST priority to schedule collaborative planning meetings.

## Co-Teaching

Two teachers engage in a professional contract to teach to a single group of students at the same time, in the same classroom, with joint accountability, although tasks and roles may vary (adapted from Friend and Cooke). The purpose is to embed the specially designed instruction to meet goals through the general education curriculum through a variety of differentiated and commonly planned teaching practices and strategies. The goal of co-teaching is small group instruction to *flexible* groups of students.

## Supported Instruction

Casual support in a classroom. Supported instruction should have a goal and be related to a child's IEP – usually the modifications and accommodations. this is *not* a good role for certified personnel, but more appropriate for paraprofessionals.

## Paraprofessional Roles in the Inclusive Classroom

Think of a paraprofessional as someone who is operating under your teaching license. Therefore, paraprofessionals require a list of tasks, pre-made modifications and data collection tools that are supplied by and planned for by the certified teachers associated with the classroom. An important part of paraprofessional support is to have (on file) a "fade back" plan to slowly shift responsibility and independence to the student with disabilities and to fade away the paraprofessional support.

## Student collaborations

Peer tutoring: two students work together. It is assumed that one student has knowledge that the other student does not have. The student with the knowledge imparts information and helps his or her peer understand the new information. This is a fluid arrangement as the knowledgeable party may be either student.

Cooperative learning: specific roles and structures that students are taught to use. Example of roles: facilitator, recorder, materials manager. Example of structures: pairs compare, pairs share, inside-outside circle. Students need to be taught how to work in groups. The fact that students are sitting as a group does not necessarily mean that they are functioning as a group. As with any strategy or skill, students should be assessed and monitored in the cooperative learning process.

## SCHEDULING TIP

### Co-Teaching

Co-teaching doesn't have to happen every day to be effective, but co-teaching every other day has been shown to be ineffective. It would be better to co-teach three days in a row—for instance, Monday, Tuesday, Wednesday and skip Thursday and Friday—than teach Monday, Wednesday, Friday and skip Tuesday and Thursday. The reason being that on Monday, the lesson may not end where it needs to in order to co-teach on Wednesday. That throws off all of the planning. Co-teaching is better in a block of time, even if it's one week on and one week off. A good collaborative inclusive program requires planning, which means two people talking to each other. If you can't or won't plan, inclusion can be very difficult.

If you need further information on co-teaching, see my book devoted to this topic: "Advancing Co-Teaching Practices: Strategies for Success" ISBN 9781468010688

# Scheduling

Special education teachers need a scheduled plan period so that they can meet with general education teachers. This is very difficult to manage if one person is trying to be an inclusion facilitator and also running self-contained classes. Those are really separate programs and separate jobs: one person provides inclusion supports, and one person teaches in the self-contained classrooms.

## Collaborative meetings

Collaboration requires that teachers meet at various points to exchange materials and ideas. Here is a real world example of how I used to set up my collaborative meetings: I was a high school resource teacher and inclusion facilitator with 28 students and 56 teachers that I needed to see on a regular basis. There was a seven period schedule and I would see teachers during plan periods on a rotating basis. For this to work, it was important the student's IEP <u>not</u> mandate him for daily support. It is <u>more</u> important to proactively plan for the student to learn at point of instruction than to be in the presence of a student daily. Therefore, I would teach student five days out of a six-day rotation. Secondly, I would take planning times graduated throughout the day and not at the same time everyday. I needed for my time to overlap with other teachers, therefore my planning time was "sprinkled" throughout my schedule. This allowed my planning time to intersect with all teachers, since at some point over the week, they had a "horizontal" time. For example, on Monday, my planning time was scheduled for the first teaching block. On Tuesday, my plan period was during second period. Wednesday, I had plan period during the third, fourth and fifth block. I had the same number of planning blocks as everybody else, but they were vertical (varied times) instead of horizontal (same time every day). See the example below:

| Monday | Tuesday | Wednesday | Thursday | Friday |
|--------|---------|-----------|----------|--------|
| Plan |  |  |  |  |
|  | Plan |  |  |  |
|  |  | Plan |  |  |
|  |  | Plan |  |  |
|  |  | Plan |  |  |
|  |  |  | Plan |  |
|  |  |  |  | Plan |

# How to Maximize Time Spent Planning
## with General Education Teachers

For these collaborative planning meetings, I set up an agenda. Now that the time was in the schedule, next we have to ensure we maximize how this time is used. (See the sample agenda on page 149.) In the meeting, the teacher and I would agree on actions to take and a time line for completion. I used a receipt book to give the teacher a copy of what we had agreed upon. At the bottom of the receipt, I wrote the who/what/time line/done information, which saved me a trip to the copier. When you have 56 teachers to meet with, you find ways to save time.

You can organize your supports in a variety of ways. However, when organizing by department, you may realize that you won't see all of the students on your caseload. There may be juniors that don't have science that year, or seniors who have already met all of their social studies requirements. In the end, you may just find it most expedient to only see the teachers you need to see and not <u>every</u> teacher on a child's schedule.

One of the questions I sometimes hear in my seminars is, "What happens to your students with disabilities when you're out consulting with the general education teachers? Where do they go?" If you're practicing an inclusive philosophy, the students will be in classrooms and you needn't worry about them. If they're in a self-contained program, then team up with another teacher to "monitor" your students while you collaborate, and then switch with that teacher on another day to afford them the same opportunity. If you're providing tutorial support in a resource room, then the students could be assigned to a one-day-a-week study hall in a study hall or assigned to another special education teacher for that particular day. One way to extend your ability to practice collaboration is to utilize "case-load sharing." Just as we expect general education teachers to collaborate with special education teachers, there should also be some "intra" departmental collaboration to help up work smarter and less harder through this process. Practice caseload sharing, which allows you to make time for planning by splitting the block period: two teachers share the room and the students, and each devotes half the period to consultation.

# Collaborative Meetings

Set up a simple agenda:

Agenda   <u>Kunkel/MacDonald</u>       Date   <u>May 3</u>

1.    Modifications for the "Survival" Project

2.    Discuss updates on the following students:   VR, LP, ST, RZ, LK

3.    Co-teaching plan lessons:          Parallel    5/12 + 5/15
                                        Stations    5/8 + 5/10

4.    ?

## Minutes and Actions

| | WHO | WHAT | TIME LINE / DONE |
|---|---|---|---|
| 1. | SK | Take PBLA and modify for Spec. Ed. students | by 5/12 |
| 2. | <u>Students:</u><br>VR*____<br>LP____<br>ST*____<br>RZ ____<br>LK ____ | <u>Missing Assignments</u><br>#2, 8, 11, Quiz 1<br>#1, Quiz 2<br><br>all set<br>#1,3,4,9,12,Quizzes 1&2 | SK to speak with students by 5/10<br>*Call parents by 5/12<br>PM call parents & set up conf. 5/10 |
| 3. | Parallel Stations | Lessons outlined in PM's plan book (she will *copy* for SK)<br>SK to plan kinesthetic activity for group 1 based on Ch. 4 of the book (survival)<br>PM to plan character analysis for group 2 and group students | |
| 4. | | PM to collect $ for dept. for secretary gift ($5)<br><br>SK to collect from Sp. Ed. | by 5/18<br><br>by 5/18      √ Done |

# Collaborative Meetings

Agenda _____ Date _____

1.

2.

3.

4.

## Minutes and Actions

| WHO | WHAT | TIME LINE / DONE |
|-----|------|------------------|

1.

2.

3.

4.

When you meet with your colleague for these collaborative meetings, make an appointment and exchange materials before you meet so that you have a purpose to your discussion. Start and end on time, and keep the personal conversation for the end of the meeting. A lot of time is wasted in meetings when people start with, 'How ya' doin'? How was the wedding last Friday?" It's tempting to get distracted by casual conversation because some of the people we work with are also our friends. However, if you can push the socializing to the end of the meeting, it will force you to get the work out of the way before you enter into socializing conversations.

## Maximizing Collaboration Time
## Ten Tips

1. Let each other know in advance what you will talk about.

2. Exchange materials before you meet.

3. Make an appointment.

4. Start and end on time.

5. Stick to work related issues, stay on task.

6. Save 5 minutes for social time at the end of the meeting, if needed.

7. Schedule your next collaborative meeting before you end.

8. Stick to a 15 to 20-minute time frame.

9. Keep a running log of your collaborative agenda as well as your meeting notes.

10. Speak from a "we" or "I" point of view and not from a "you" point of view.

The last point is very important: What are WE going to do to provide support? How are WE going to divvy this up? How should WE modify the test? Should I take a section? Should WE do this together? Are WE both comfortable doing this? It needs to be a collaborative or shared conversation between two professionals, a conversation that underscores shared ownership of the tasks and the students.

# Co-Teaching

My preferred way to support students is via the co-teaching model. I began co-teaching in middle schools in the 1980s and then spent ten years co-teaching at the high school level.

According to Dr. Marilyn Friend, "Co-teaching is a service delivery option of two or more educators or other certified staff that contract to share instructional responsibility for a single group of students. This is done primarily in one classroom or workspace for a specific content. The co-teachers share mutual ownership, pooled resources and joint accountability for the group of students, although each individual teacher's level of participation may vary."

Let's chunk this definition for clarity:

*Co-teaching is a service delivery option of two or more educators or other certified staff that contract to share instructional responsibility for a single group of students.*

Co-teaching is one group of students in one classroom. It's not the history class and the English class coming together to form an American studies class with fifty students. Co-teaching is accomplished primarily in one classroom or workspace for a specific content. It's not a special education teacher showing up and taking the special education students down the hallway - that's just teaching in two places. Co-teaching is in one classroom space. There are some exceptions to that. One day, you might take half the class to the library to work on a project while the other half stays back to work on a research prompt or a lab. The next day, you switch roles.

*Co teachers share mutual ownership, pooled resources and joint accountability for the group of students, although each individual teacher's level of participation may vary.*

A special education teacher may teach general education classes if co-teaching with a general education teacher. Participation may vary based on the special education teacher's expertise in the content, or the general education teacher's comfort level with allowing the other teacher to teach the content. As long as there is a student with identified special education needs in the classroom, there is something in the law called incidental benefits: if the other students benefit from the efforts of a special educator, so be it. When you bring twice the amount of content expertise together, it creates a very dynamic learning situation.

School administrators often state that if they're paying for two teachers, they want to see twice the amount of instruction in that class, which is absolutely right. Co-teaching should not be set up as though one person is the teacher and the other person is a helper. Two professionals provide multiple opportunities to respond, increased assessment, more feedback, targeted instruction and reduced student-teacher ratio.

One of the first questions we have to ask ourselves is, "Can we make this a voluntary arrangement?" If co-teaching can be voluntary, that's ideal. However, in the real world, co-teachers are simply assigned to each other. If that happens, especially when the teachers are new to each other, the most important first step to take at the beginning of the school year is to have a conversation.

Co-teaching is not establishing a teacher and a helper. In order to deliver instruction and share joint accountability, teachers must learn to communicate their ideas and preferences.

> **Co-teaching is sharing mutual ownership, pooled resources and joint accountability for a single group of students.**

As they advance their practices, educators move through stages of co-teaching.

Stage 1 is typified by:

> ➢ Teachers presenting separate lessons
> ➢ One teacher assumes the role of "boss" and the other of "helper."
> ➢ Presentations tend to be traditional in nature.

Stage 2 is a transition phase characterized by:

> ➢ Lesson structuring and presentation begins to be shared by both teachers.
> ➢ Both teachers direct some of the activities.
> ➢ The special educator often offers mini-lessons or clarifies strategies.
> ➢ Presentations begin to vary in instructional style, learning styles, and differentiated practices.
> ➢ "Chalk" passes freely between teachers.

Stage 3 uses more advanced practices, and can be identified by:

> ➢ Both teachers comfortably participate in the presentation of the lesson, provide instruction, and structure the learning activities.
> ➢ Students address questions and discuss concerns with both teachers.
> ➢ Flexible small group instruction, such as station or parallel groups, are the predominant configurations used for instruction.
> ➢ Strategies, differentiated instruction, multiple intelligences, tiered lessons and learning styles instruction are embedded throughout the lesson on a regular basis.
> ➢ IEP strategies are embedded as specially designed instruction in the general education classroom.

# Co-Teaching: Roles

Consider this question for a moment: if you could be cloned, what could two of you accomplish simultaneously in the classroom?

What could you accomplish if there were two of you in a single class?

| Teacher A's responsibilities | Teacher B's responsibilities |
|---|---|
| | |

Here are a few ideas that teachers in my national seminars have suggested they would do if there were two of them in the classroom:

➢ Go halvesies with paperwork, responsibilities, lesson planning, etc.

➢ Break up the class into smaller groups and simultaneously present a lesson.

➢ One teacher teaches while the other teacher evaluates the students to determine whether they're getting or not getting it: observing, checking in with students to see what they know, and troubleshooting.

# Parity: Contracting to Share Instructional Responsibility for a Single Group of Students

The number one strategy to ensure successful co-teaching for any situation is parity. Some questions to discuss with your co-teacher before you begin:

1. How will we establish parity among ourselves and with our students?

2. How will we plan?

3. How will roles be determined?

4. What about grading, parent phone calls, IEP meetings, communications with guidance or administration?

5. What will we tell the students, parents, and other staff?

6. How will we handle various behaviors in the classroom?

7. What bugs you the most?

8. What routines work best for you?

9. What do you like to do the best, your successes?

10. What tasks do you hate to do?

11. When will we plan?

12. Will we keep one plan book?

13. How will we set up the room?

14. Will both teachers have adult size furniture in the room?

15. How will we both work with all students?

Below are examples of the teaching methods for Level 1 and Level 2 practices.
GOAL: To operate at Level 2 for 70% or more of the time.

## Co-Teaching

### Level 1 Practices: Whole Group Instruction
### (30% or less of your co-teaching time)
  - Speak and Add
  - Speaker and Writer
  - One Teach, One Facilitate
  - One Teach, One Assess
  - One Teach, One Take Data
  - One Teach, One Support
  - One Teach, One Handle Materials
  - Two Facilitate (whole group)
  - Turn Taking (teachers in front of the room together)
  - Cooperative learning groups with one or two teacher facilitation

### Level 2 Practices: Small Flexible Groupings
### (70% or more of your classroom co-teaching time)
  - Parallel or Mirror Lessons (same style)
  - Parallel or Mirror Lessons (differentiated styles)
  - Parallel or Mirror Lessons (learning styles)
  - Two station Flip Flop
  - Two station Pre-teach and Enrich
  - Three station rotation
  - Three stations, tiered
  - Four station rotation
  - Four stations with Flip/Flop
  - Skills Groups
  - Enrichment Groups
  - Pre-teaching Groups
  - Re-teaching Groups
  - Assessment/Progress Monitoring Groups
  - Six stations with interrupters

### Important tips for setting up Level 2 practices
  1. Agree on room arrangement
  2. Plan materials
  3. Include kinesthetic activities
  4. Pre-determine switch times and which teacher will be in charge of "the clock."
  5. Discuss management of independent groups.

# Practices for Level 1 and Level 2

There are two kinds of groups: those that are teacher-led instructional groups and the cooperative learning groups, which have an independent task. Co-teaching at Level 2 consists of teacher-led groups wherein each teacher is instructing a smaller group of students focused on a data-derived instructional objective. Student needs for accommodations, modifications, and specially designed instruction are embedded into the small group lesson. At Level 1, teachers facilitate general whole group learning. At Level 2, the practices focus on specific instructional presentation in small groups. It is extremely important that the instructional groups not be consistently homogeneous. Take advantage of differentiated practices to flexibly group students.

Treat your co-teacher's different teaching style as an advantage rather than a conflict to be solved. It's important to be flexible in order to capitalize on the talents that each teacher brings to the table. One teacher may be more traditional in style. The other may be a free spirit. In differentiated instruction, there is room for multiple approaches.

## Level 1 Practices

Speak and Add
Both teachers are at the front of the classroom. One person is speaking, and the other person is clarifying key points in the lesson.

Speaker and Writer
One person speaks and the other person writes and records. This can be combined with the previous practice, which then becomes Speak and Add and Write.

One Teach, One Facilitate
One teacher teaches and the other teacher walks around the class, checking on students.

This is my least favorite of all teaching configurations. It tends to be overused due to a lack of planning and a lack of clarity about what co-teaching is. A little bit of help during guided practice is all right. However, there is more we can do that will utilize teaching expertise for maximum student benefit. You must be cautious with this approach, as it has major negative side effects over time.

One Teach, One Assess
One teacher teaches while the other teacher assesses. For example, while one teacher is teaching, the other can pull three or four kids aside and give them a one-minute mini quiz on the top five questions that are going to be on the test, to see who knows them and who needs more help.

"What's the answer for this? What do you know about that?" You can check off how many questions the students got right. If they didn't know the answers, you have the necessary information to form small, flexible groups the next day so that you can pre-teach them what they missed.

## One Teach, One Support

One teacher teaches while the other supports students. Usually, you see one teacher sitting down next to a student. This is a configuration that can create enabled student behaviors if it is overused.

## Two Facilitate, Whole Group

This configuration is used during guided practice or during cooperative learning groups.

## Turn Taking

One teacher teaches while the other teacher remains 'dormant,' then teachers switch roles. You have to be careful with this approach, as it can look like job sharing if done incorrectly.

## Level 2 Practices

To describe some of these practices I waved my magic wand and created an imaginary co-teacher named Lenora, who is a terrific co-teacher. She communicates well and trusts me as her co-teacher. She has a positive outlook from which all students can learn. She is flexible and willing to do whatever it takes to ensure student achievement.

### Parallel or Mirror Lessons (same style)

Say that Lenora and I are going to co-teach math and today we're teaching fractions.

We take our class of thirty students and we split them down the middle. We arrange the groups so that Lenora and I have eye contact. We can see what's going on with each other, and it helps us with pacing. We teach the exact same lesson the same way to two small groups of students (15 in each group).

### TEACHING TIP

**Q&A – Parallel Lessons**

Q: What do you do with kids who are distracted by two teachers talking at the same time during parallel lessons?

A: Say that Tommy Turnaround is with Lenora, but he's paying attention to my lesson. There are two options: either move Tommy to the group that attracts his interest, or leave him be and let him turn around to pay attention to the other (exact same) lesson. Either way, he ends up learning the lesson.

See pages 164-166 for visuals that represent the following ideas:

<u>Parallel or Mirror Lessons</u> (differentiated styles)
For this practice, we still have our two groups, but now we're going to differentiate our teaching styles. Lenora's going to teach using one process and I'm going to teach focusing on a different process. We differentiated our processes, but we're still covering the same material

<u>Parallel or Mirror Lessons</u> (learning styles)
We teach the same lesson, grouping students by learning style strengths. Lenora is going to lecture (auditory) and I'm going to create an activity (kinesthetic) for students to learn the same material to the same level of specificity.

In this example, we have tiered it: Lenora got the kids that are ready for the skill and I teach the kids that need a little pre-teaching first.

**TEACHING TIP**

**Differentiation**

For differentiation, begin by pre-assessing your students. Use the pre-assessment information to either tier your activity or make it a choice activity.

<u>Two Station Flip/Flop</u>
In this example, Lenora and I are teaching two interrelated skills. Lenora is teaching vocabulary and I'm teaching writing process. After twenty minutes, we're going to flip flop – her students are going to come to me, and mine are going to go to her.

<u>Two Group Pre-Teach Enrich Switch</u>
Let's say that Lenora and I have pre-assessed our students' ability to reduce common fractions.
  ➢ I am going to pre-teach the group that isn't quite ready for the lesson.
  ➢ Lenora, the content teacher, is going to teach the lesson on reducing fractions.

After twenty minutes, the groups are going to switch.

  ➢ My group goes to Lenora and she teaches the same lesson on reducing fractions to the second group that had received pre-teaching.
  ➢ Lenora's group comes to me and I either re-teach or enrich the group that received the content lesson first.
One group needed more information before entering into the lesson, and one group was able to get re-teaching, or go beyond the lesson.

## Three Station Rotation
Two stations are teacher-taught, and there is an independent station. At a timed interval, the groups switch. For example: one group is learning key content with Lenora, one group is learning vocabulary with me, and the independent group is learning through a Pass the Problem activity (see page 163). After fifteen minutes, the kids rotate to the next station. The kids can be grouped by the criteria you consider most important.

What's nice about this configuration is that the opportunities to respond are doubled. In a whole group class, you ask a question, students raise their hands to answer, and you call on one student. Small group instruction is a way to increase opportunities to respond. We co-teach because we have certain students in the classroom who have trouble learning. In a large group, those kids don't always like to respond because they are embarrassed or unsure of their answers. In small groups, they are more likely to respond because it is safer and more intimate.

## Three Station Tiers
Students are assigned to ability level groups. Students remain with their groups and teachers rotate to give groups mini-lessons.

## Four Stations Mini-Lessons
There are two teacher-led stations where the students receive mini-lessons, and two independent stations. Students are equally divided into four groups and rotate based on a pre-determined timed fashion. For example, in a 40-minute lesson block, students would spend ten minutes at each of the four stations.

## Four Station Flip/Flop
Each teacher is responsible for only two groups of students, for a total of four groups. Teacher one teaches his/her first group and then switches and teaches his/her second group. Teacher two does the same. This allows for a variety of focused skill development. For example, in a 40-minute lesson block, each teacher will see only two groups for 20 minutes each.

## Skills Groups
These are small groups we put together based on specific criteria. Maybe you have reviewed test scores and you form groups to focus on specific items students missed. These are short-term quick groups. You might work with four particular kids on one specific issue for five minutes, then return them to the mix and get four more kids. It's a way of targeting instruction that kids need. It could be the same skill for each group, or it could be individualized, based on kids who have different needs.

## Enrichment Groups
Take opportunities for one teacher to work with students on extending or enriching the curriculum.

## Re-Teaching

Re-teach materials students did not master. There are all kinds of re-teaching opportunities, which are needed to clarify or pinpoint instructional deficits and/or student needs.

### Pre-Teaching for Success

Pre-teach concepts or pre-teach the lesson. Kids arrive at the classroom and there's a "Do Now" activity on the board. But in any class, there are always about five fidgety kids that take two minutes to sit down, and another five minutes to find their pencils, and another four minutes to pick their heads up. By that time, they have successfully manipulated their way out of doing the warm-up activity. Preemptively grab those five kids and provide pre-teaching of the lesson.

That way, when the whole group receives the lesson, the pre-taught kids can enter the lesson with confidence and experience success.

## Assessment-Progress Monitoring

Evaluate student competency with material by conducting mini-assessments. These can be oral or written opportunities.

## Six Stations with Interrupters

Interrupters are mini teaching opportunities that help to clarify a point. They take less than two minutes and usually include videos or dramatic elements.

Think of interrupters as a commercial that occurs while students transition between stations. For a six-station configuration, I recommend they occur every other rotation. That is, interrupters will occur three times during the six rotations.

Try this practice for multi-faceted lessons. This configuration also works well for block schedules or multiple day lessons.

Instructions for this practice are on the following page.

Six Stations with Interrupters instructions:

To implement this practice, create two teacher stations and four independent stations. Here is one example of how you might set up this co-teaching configuration:

> Station 1 is a teaching station where students receive direct instruction.
> Station 2 is independent reading, where students will read something, take some notes and respond to questions.
> Station 3 is an independent group – these students are writing a commercial based on an assigned topic. They have to come up with a 2-minute skit (or commercial) that highlights some of the key points that we've discussed.
> Station 4 is a teaching station for students to receive additional direct instruction from the second teacher.
> Station 5 is an independent station. The students have laptop computer work to do.
> Station 6 is a standing station. Students have concept cards and they have to sort them into different categories, as a pair.

Six Stations with Interrupters example:

Imagine one rotating student named Susan.

> Susan receives instruction from the teacher at Station 1.
> After about fifteen minutes, she and the group rotate to the reading assignment at Station 2.
> Then we have a commercial break or interrupter. The students that were in Station 3 get up and do a two-minute commercial with some of the key ideas they were exposed to. They present to the entire class for two minutes. Susan watches.
> Susan rotates to Station 3 and she works on her commercial break.
> After fifteen minutes, she rotates to Station 4 for some teacher-led learning.
> We stop again, and there is another commercial break put on by some of the students. Susan's group performs their commercial for the class.
> Susan rotates to Station 5, then to Station 6, and then there is a third commercial break.

Research has shown that the interrupters give the brain an opportunity to absorb information. It doesn't have to be a commercial that students devise. Maybe you have a brief Internet video that illustrates key points of the lesson. It could be something humorous that breaks up the day. By providing opportunities to move around, you have included kinesthetic teaching.

Ultimately, it's the curriculum that determines which configurations are most effective. Working in collaboration, teachers consider what needs to be taught and then find the best way to teach the content.

# SPECIAL STRATEGY

## Pass the Problem

Usage: Small group constructive independent work – for Level 2 Co-teaching

The best way to advance your co-teaching practices is to work in small groups. To help you envision how to advance co-teaching, here is a simple procedure that I call Pass the Problem.

Imagine a classroom with 30 children, divided into three groups. Teacher 1 will work with the first group on vocabulary. Teacher 2 will work with the second group on some important academic area. And the third group, the independent group, is going to participate in the Pass the Problem activity.

### How to implement this strategy

For a group of 10 students, you will need:

10 white boards

10 dry erase markers

10 dry erasers

1 wet erase marker (the type used with overhead projectors, for example)

1 two-minute egg timer

3 x 5 index cards

10 related problems to solve

### How to set up Pass the Problem

If you were using this strategy for a math class, you would first devise 10 math problems that are similar in nature or that practice the same skill, but in 10 different ways. You write the problem on the top half of the white board with the wet erase marker. On the back of each board, you tape a 3 x 5 inch card with the answer to the problem.

### How to conduct Pass the Problem

The independent study group students are each given one board, a dry erase marker and an eraser.

The two-minute timer is set by one student to indicate to students to begin solving the problem on their board. The students use the dry erase markers to practice the problem on the bottom half of the board. At the end of two minutes, everyone turns their board over and takes half a minute or so to compare the answer on the 3 x 5 card with their own solution to the problem. They correct their answers and when they're done, they erase their work on the bottom of the boards. The original problem that was written with the wet erase marker remains. The students pass the problem to the student sitting to their right and the timer is reset.

# Diagrams of Co-Teaching Configurations

## Mirror
### (2 groups)

Each teacher teaches the **same objective at the same time (groups do not switch)**

| Teacher 1 Group A | Teacher 2 Group B |

### Variations

- **Vary** groups through the use of **Differentiation**
- Apply different **Teaching Styles**
- Each group offers different **Learning Styles** or **Multiple Intelligences** options
- Vary by using differentiated **Assessments**

## Flip/Flop
### (2 groups)

After a timed interval, groups switch from one teacher to the other.

Two Objectives. Each teacher teaches a **Different Objective to their group**

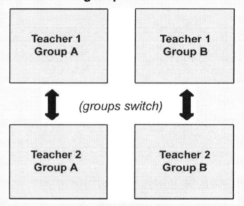

*(groups switch)*

### Variation

- Specific skill stations without flip/flop (2 different objectives based on data)

## Flip/Flop Switch
### (2 groups)

Two or three teaching objectives

Data based groups. Teacher 1 teaches the main lesson, Teacher 2 PRE-teaches the lesson. After an interval, groups switch.

The pre-taught group then receives the same lesson from Teacher 1.

The lesson group receives RE-teaching or ENRICHMENT from Teacher 2.

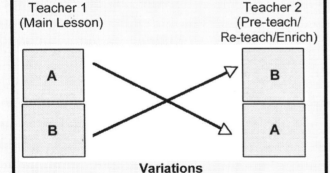

### Variations

- Each group receives initial pre-teaching lesson based on data-driven decisions.
- Students receive initial lesson (mirror style) then students are regrouped for re-teaching purposes.

## 3 Station Rotation
### (3 groups: two teacher groups and one independent group)

Three teaching objectives

Each teacher instructs a group, and a third group completes an independent activity. After a timed interval, the groups switch. The students participate in all three groups.

*Note: In the independent group, students may work or sit: alone, in pairs, or as a group.*

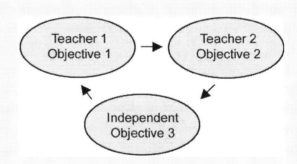

### Variations

Three stations, but students only participate in two groups, with the following determined by the data:

- One teacher group and one independent group
- Two teacher groups, no independent group

| **3 Station Tiers** | **4 Station Rotation** |
|---|---|
| (3 groups: all teacher taught for some time) | (4 groups: 2 teacher taught, 2 independent) |

**3 Station Tiers**

One objective, tiered for maximum student success (NO Rotation)

Teacher 1 teaches the basic group (example: 20 minutes), Teacher 2 splits the same amount of time between the two other groups (example: 10 minutes teaching the intermediate group / then 10 minutes teaching the advanced group - teaching is alternated with independent work)

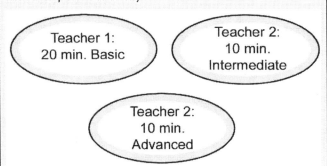

**Variation**

• Teacher 1 spends 20 minutes enriching the advanced group and Teacher 2 spends 10 minutes teaching the other two groups.

**4 Station Rotation**

Four objectives
Students spend time with each teacher and complete/participate in two independent tasks.

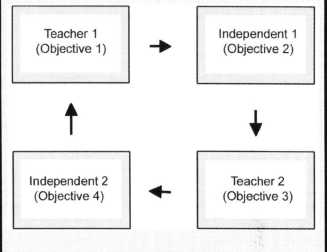

**Variation**

• Students may complete the rotations over two days instead of one.

---

**4 Stations with one Teacher Flip/flop**
(4 groups)

Two Objectives

The class is spit in half and each teacher alternates between an instructional group and an independent group. Students only see one teacher.

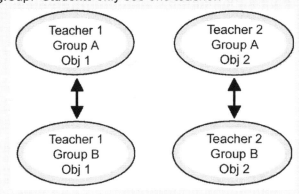

**Variations**

• Teachers have the same objective for each group
• Teachers have different objectives for each group based on student needs.

**4 Stations with Tiers**
(4 groups)

One objective (NO rotation by students)

Each group works with a teacher for a specified amount of time, then the teacher moves to a second group. The lesson content is the same, but the lesson is differentiated for the various ability group levels.

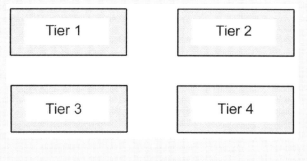

**Variation**

• You may have one basic, two intermediate and one advanced group or any other ability combinations that make sense.

| **6 Stations with Interrupters**<br>(6 groups) | **Skills Groups**<br>(1 large group task and<br>2 small flexible mini groups) |
|---|---|

Six Objectives

Students rotate between six groups. Two are teacher taught and four are independent. This configuration may take more than one class period if you do not work in a block schedule.

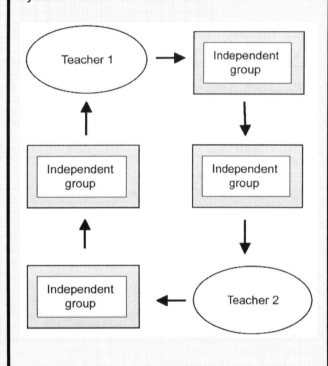

Objectives vary by group (many objectives: individualized)

Students are given a whole group task. Each teacher siphons off one to six students at a time to offer a short (in duration) mini lesson. Students are then returned to the group at large and another mini lesson group is created.

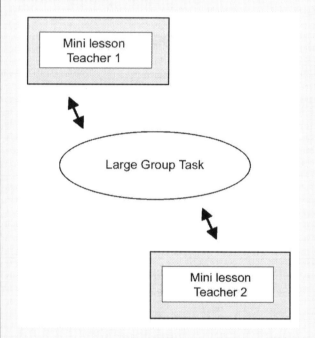

### Variations

• Students may double up in one group, or skip a group if it is appropriate.

### Variations

• The purpose of the group may include re-teaching, pre-teaching, conferencing, assessment, skill focus, collaboration, drill, behavioral practice or any other need, as determined by the teachers. Each group has its own purpose, make-up and duration.

# REASONS WHY CO-TEACHING WILL WORK:

- Develop relationships
- Structure
- Immediate rewards
- Shared planning and evaluation
- Easier to communicate with parents
- Learn from each other
- Easer to teach when sub is in
- Less boring
- Shared accountability
- Two heads are better than one
- It's fun
- Different personalities to reach different kids
- Shared responsibility
- Motivating
- Inclusion is a right
- Content is shared
- Climate is improved
- Kids feel better about school
- Adults feel better about school
- Students become accepting
- Parents become more interested
- Students learn from each other
- Strategies are mixed with content
- More creativity
- Easier to do behavior modification programs
- Special education teacher has a better idea of required work and students' status

- General education teacher supported continually
- Cooperative strategies help all learn
- Consultation helps with problem-solving
- All students benefit from strategies
- Presentation variety
- More opportunity for different grouping activities
- Less chance a kid falls through cracks
- Fresher ideas
- Parallel Teaching
- Peer tutoring
- More modeling
- Increased humor
- Meet more students' needs
- Save $$
- Increased resources
- Better use of teachers strengths Teaching teams work
- Tolerance
- Frustration
- Shared knowledge

- Requires less building space
- Smaller teacher/student ratio
- More personal
- Distribution of work load
- Supervision of students is better
- Kids taught to strength areas

# Planning for Co-Teaching

*If you're going to co-teach, you must co-plan.*

Work with your administrator to determine how to create co-planning time. One possible scenario is this: the general education teacher has study hall and the special education teacher has planning during the same period. You need blocks of time for mega planning, whereas some of the finer details can be worked out in snippets of time – in the lunchroom, on the way to your cars in the parking lot, and so on.

A unit planning worksheet will help you keep track of the co-teaching strategies you use to help students achieve educational goals. On page 171, there is an example of a unit planning worksheet used for a high school physics class. On page 172, there is a blank reproducible form for you to use however it best suits your purpose.

## Finding the Time to Collaborate and to Co-plan

Meeting once a month will probably yield ten co-teaching ideas, which may be enough to fill a 10-month cycle. If it isn't possible to include planning in your schedule, here are some ideas that will help you find the time:

➢ **Hire substitutes.** Floating subs can be available on a rotating bi-weekly basis for collaboration and co-planning to occur. Subs can cover duties and non-instructional responsibilities.

Two subs can be hired to come in on the same day once a month – not for a particular class, but for flotation duty. Teachers could sign up to have a sub cover their classes. However, the sub should cover a duty period and not a classroom, otherwise the teachers would have to plan for the sub coming so that they could go out and plan, which doesn't make much sense. Perhaps a film could be shown that day, or some other activity that would not require major league instructions.

➢ **Use of interns.** Internships are becoming very popular on college campuses. Less than the cost of an aide, interns are generally seniors or post-graduates who are fulfilling their college requirements before they begin student teaching. Interns can be used for coverage.

➢ **Volunteers.** Parents and school volunteers can help in two ways: they can either provide coverage or act as a guest speaker. Arrange with a volunteer committee to have guest speakers come in once a month and speak to the class about a career related to your current curriculum. Meanwhile, you can sit at the back of the class and get some planning done.

➢ **Technology.** Make full use of the convenience that technology offers – communicate with your co-teacher by phone, fax, e-mail or Skype.

- ➤ **Paraprofessionals.** Use paraprofessionals to monitor a practice assignment for 15 minutes while you meet in the back of the room to plan.

- ➤ **Schedule it.** Volunteer to be on the schedule committee in your school, which gives you a voice in the decision-making process. Try to arrange plan time with your co-teacher. Should your co-teacher have a duty period such as study hall at the same time as your plan time, you could agree to meet in study hall once a week.

- ➤ **Before or after school.** Meet before or after school once a week or once every other week, depending on your curriculum demands.

- ➤ **One teacher covers two classes.** A teacher in your department or team shows a film all students need to watch. You combine classes and alternate coverage during the film time to free one of you up to meet with another teacher.

- ➤ **Other professionals teach a class.** Guidance department meets with your class to cover their developmental guidance curriculum or the school social worker does a lesson on problem solving.

- ➤ **Professional development time.** Use some of your professional development time to create co-taught units.

- ➤ **Use existing planning time.**

- ➤ **Rethink faculty meetings.** Are there some items that can be bulleted in a memo, freeing up 15 minutes for collaboration and co-planning to occur?

- ➤ **Summer curriculum writing.** Is this available for you to use to plan or collaborate to preset the year? Can you write a curriculum that will be based on two teachers in the classroom?

- ➤ **Release time.**

- ➤ **Lunch together?**

- ➤ **Found time.** Snow days, assemblies.

- ➤ **Student teacher.** Intern?

# Co-Planning Tips

1. Set up a schedule time and stick to it.

2. Map out the unit in advance on a calendar, then zoom in on specific co-taught lessons that need a lot of planning together (i.e. parallel or teaming).

3. Vary your co-teaching configurations.

4. Let the curriculum drive what co-teaching arrangements make sense for a given lesson.

5. Schedule in your co-planning time before anything else...keep it sacred!

6. Send each other your ideas in advance (notes, e-mail, etc.) so you are not starting from scratch.

7. Try to plan about two weeks at a time. Review your plans weekly and make adjustments as necessary.

8. It is <u>smarter</u> and <u>easier</u> to plan advanced small group configurations that improve test scores than it is to plan for a whole group. Save time and improve scores by only planning for two, three or four-group configurations in which each teacher <u>teaches</u> a separate group at a time. **Remember, if you don't co-plan... you can't co-teach.**

## TEACHING TIP

**Parallel Teaching**

When you're parallel teaching, something to avoid is having groups end at different times, because the idle group tends to become chatty, and that can distract the other groups in the room. In order to pace your lessons so that you end on time, a useful tool is the Teach Timer. The new model has a built-in projector, and it's available from:

http://www.schoolmart.com/teachtimer2.aspx

**Unit Planning Worksheet: High School Physics**

Co-teaching

| Date | Content | Skills | Assessment | Co-teaching Approach | Modifications Needed |
|------|---------|--------|------------|----------------------|----------------------|
| September | Measuring systems | Make measurement in SI units | Written lab reports | Station teaching | Measurement guide |
| | Uncertainties in Measurement | Present the results of an experiment as a lab report | Tests: problems, multiple choice, essay | Alternative teaching | Large graph paper |
| | Vector addition | Add vectors using trig | | | |
| | | Use significant figures in collecting and manipulating data | Lab performance | | |
| | | Analyze graphs of date for slope and the equation of the line | | | |
| October | Linear motion | Vector addition continued | Written lab reports | Alternative teaching | Oral lab reports |
| | Vector addition | Analyze the effect of forces on motion | | | |
| | Acceleration of gravity | Use algebra to solve equations for motion | Tests | Parallel teaching | Assigned groups |
| | | Represent the motion of a body as position vs. Time and velocity vs. Time graphs from lab data | Lab performance | | |
| | | | Scientists report | | |
| | | Determine the acceleration of gravity in the lab | Oral presentation of group problem-solving activity | | |

Reproducible
# Co-Teaching Planner

| Date | Content | Skills | Assessment | Co-Teaching Approach | Roles | Modification Needs |
|------|---------|--------|------------|---------------------|-------|--------------------|
|      |         |        |            |                     |       |                    |
|      |         |        |            |                     |       |                    |
|      |         |        |            |                     |       |                    |

# Four station rotation: mini lesson – lesson planner, Level 2

| Station 1 | Station 2 | Station 3 | Station 4 |
|---|---|---|---|
| Timing: | Timing: | Timing: | Timing: |
| Directions: | Directions: | Directions | Directions: |
| Objective: | Objective: | Objective: | Objective: |
| Group: | Group: | Group: | Group: |
| Teacher's Role/ Independent Instructions: | Teacher's Role/ Independent Instructions: | Teacher's Role/ Independent Instructions: | Teacher's Role/ Independent Instructions: |
| Description of activity or lesson plan | Description of activity or lesson plan | Description of activity or lesson plan | Description of activity or lesson plan |

# The Paraprofessional

A team meeting may result in the decision to make paraprofessionals available to support inclusion. Here are some questions to consider regarding paraprofessionals:

**What can a paraprofessional do and not do in my classroom?** This can vary greatly from school to school and class to class. Generally speaking, as long as a teacher plans instruction, a paraprofessional can be given directions to instruct students. However, many districts have various degrees of paraprofessional, union standards, policies and procedures that may outline this more thoroughly.

Paraprofessionals can modify under the direction of both general and special educators. Paraprofessionals aren't supposed to create modifications all by themselves, because that involves and a keen understanding of the student's IEP. A paraprofessional can be used to work with any student in the classroom. If the paraprofessional only attends to one or two students or appears attached to the student by sitting next to him, it can almost seem as though a force field has been created around the student with disabilities that prevents true inclusion in the classroom community. Paraprofessionals are an extension of the teacher(s) in the classroom. It should not be expected that the paraprofessional is "in charge" of the student with significant learning needs. This is the duty of certified staff.

**What is the best way to use a paraprofessional?** It is best to use the paraprofessional to augment instruction by using flexible groupings in a classroom. A paraprofessional should work with all children in the classroom to help create a more inclusive environment.

**How do I supervise a paraprofessional...is it my responsibility?** As a general education teacher, it is your job to provide any paraprofessional with direction in your classroom. The paraprofessional may need plans, materials or grouping assignments. As a special education teacher, your job is to work collaboratively with the paraprofessional and the teacher to ensure that the IEP is being met and that the paraprofessional is used to support instruction in the classroom and is not merely taking notes or wandering around without a purpose.

**If a paraprofessional is assigned as a 1:1, can or should that paraprofessional work with other students? YES!!** On occasion a student will arrive in the classroom with a one-on-one paraprofessional. Inclusion best practice dictates that the paraprofessional be available for the entire classroom, not just one student. That is, unless there's a serious behavioral issue, such as a biter or chair thrower who needs to stay within a certain circle of safety, or a medical issue that dictates the need for constant proximity, a paraprofessional is an assistant to the teacher, not a substitute for the student working with the teacher. Constant paraprofessional proximity does communicate a non-verbal message of helplessness. Paraprofessionals are intended to be available for students, but are not meant to be their eyes and ears.

So unless there is an issue with safety or imminent health concerns, the paraprofessional should work with any and all students that he or she can help in the classroom. While the paraprofessional works with some of the general education students in the class, the teacher is then free to work with students who have special needs. You want to avoid the appearance of a paraprofessional that is "attached" to the student with an IEP.

**What do you do if a paraprofessional doesn't do what the teacher asks?** Generally, most paraprofessionals will do whatever you need them to do. If a paraprofessional is hired to provide support in your classroom, one of the first things you should do is to sit down and have a conversation. "This is what support looks like in my classroom, and this is how we're going to accomplish it together." Offer the paraprofessional a list of the kinds of things you might request, so that they understand up front what to expect. It can be difficult to introduce a new responsibility midway through the school year. It's better to be proactive than reactive, and a conversation and a job description will generally forestall miscommunication and conflict. However, if by the second day of school the paraprofessional doesn't agree with the job description, then send the paraprofessional to talk with your administrator. What's the point of having paraprofessionals if they're not going to provide support that best meets a student's needs and engages the student in learning?

Often, teachers dislike supervising because that's not their specialty. Nevertheless, if you're a general educator with a paraprofessional assigned to your classroom, even if that paraprofessional is paid for through special education, you're going to have to wear a supervisory hat to some degree. Remember, the paraprofessional is acting under your monitoring in your classroom. Their actions should enhance the learning in your classroom, not create learning problems such as enabled behaviors. If you have doubts about parameters, you can sit down with the special education department and ask what types of assignments the paraprofessional can handle. Take your list and ask if each item is appropriate, then hammer out an agreement before meeting with the paraprofessional. Also, remember to be informed regarding job descriptions, working agreements and bargaining unit specifications.

If you need further information on co-teaching,
see my book devoted to this topic:
"Advancing Co-Teaching Practices: Strategies for Success"
ISBN 9781468010688

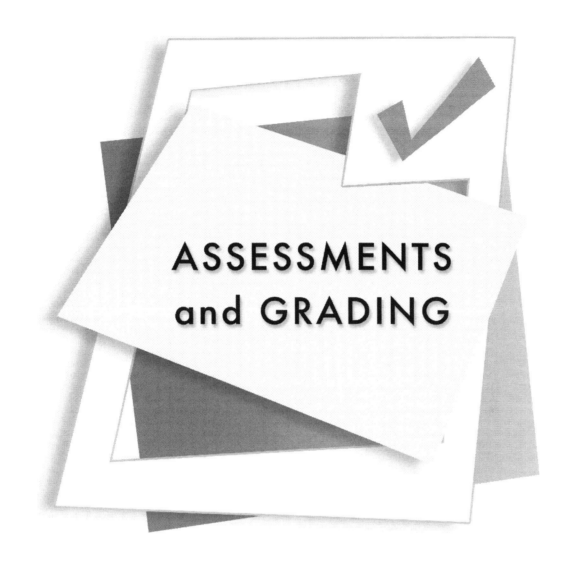

# ASSESSMENTS and GRADING

## Demonstrating Competency

The purpose of a test or quiz is to find out what a student has learned. For a student with disabilities to demonstrate competency, standard testing methods may not apply, or may not be the best approach to unlock and progress monitor what the student has learned.

For instance, if you have a student who has a documented memory disability, it may not make sense to administer a test that requires memorization skills. Testing that student's memory may only certify their disability and not provide assessment insight into their competency with the materials. We have to look to alternative methods to determine whether the student is competent in the material. There are a variety of non-traditional methods that can be used to monitor progress and to gauge a student's growth.

Nevertheless, the reality created by high stakes testing is that we will probably never get completely away from certain types of tests. Students' ability to take the high stakes tests may determine whether they receive a diploma or not. In the following pages, you'll find some ideas for accommodating and modifying tests, as well as some alternative methods that may be used to determine a student's competency.

# Modifying Tests and Quizzes

<u>Before</u> you modify a test or quiz, collaborate with your colleagues regarding these questions:

1. **What is the purpose of this test/quiz?**

2. **Is this test or quiz the only way this student can demonstrate competency in this subject matter?**

3. **Is it necessary for the student to demonstrate competency in all the material?**

4. **What type of modification does this student receive?**

Your answers to the above questions should guide you in accommodating and modifying tests and quizzes.

# The Purpose of Tests and Quizzes:
## A Guide to Demonstrating Competency

➤ If the purpose of the test or quiz is to memorize certain facts, then consider the different supports required by modification type.

➤ If the purpose of a test or quiz is to rate how well a student understands a concept, can the student simply tell you everything he or she knows about the material? This is usually graded via a checklist or rubric to see if the information contains the important points.

➤ If the purpose for the test is to qualify a student for the next level (say, math or a world language), look to accommodations that support the student. For example: extended time, a writer, a reader, enlarged print, use of assistive/adaptive technology or calculator.

➤ If the purpose of the test is to give a grade at the end of a unit, then ask yourself if there is a way the student could earn a culminating grade by tapping an area of strength. For example: at the end of an Egypt unit, the student produces a model of a pyramid, presents the model to the class, and develops a worksheet for classmates to complete about the interior shafts of a popular pyramid.

➤ If the purpose of the content is to demonstrate an understanding of a survey of information, then allow the student to complete a series of projects from a menu of choice. For example, the student has studied various novels around the theme of survival. The student is then given a menu and chooses one item to complete from column A, one from column B, etc.

# Modifying Tests and Quizzes
## Type 1 Ideas

Here are some strategies for accommodating tests and quizzes for the Type 1 learner.

## Modifying Structure

1. Print the information.

2. Use a lot of white space.

3. DO NOT USE ALL CAPITAL LETTERS.

4. Place one section of the test per page.

5. Place point value at the end of every section.

6. Allow the student to write on the test.

7. Enlarge blanks. Especially for students who have grapho-motor issues and writing difficulties, larger blanks can make a difference. Little tiny blanks are just harder for some students to manage.

8. Keep blanks uniform in size. Sometimes, to make a test nice and neat, teachers will end blanks on a margin. The first blank might be large, the next blank might be smaller; but here is what students with disabilities think: "Okay, that first blank is large, therefore my teacher wants me to use a phrase or a large word. This blank is small, therefore I need a small word."

9. Don't use dashes. Students will count the number of dashes and try to figure out a word that has that many letters in it.

10. Type the test, and use a 14 pt font that is easy to read, such as Arial.

## Accommodating Directions

➢ Read the directions chorally with the students.

➢ Read the directions twice.

➢ Bullet the directions on the page.

➢ Highlight, bold, or underline key terms.

➢ Capitalize all absolute words (never, always), as well as any other important words.

➢ Keep directions to a minimum. Remember that students have a hard time following more than two-step directions when they have processing issues.

➢ Define complicated words in the directions.

➢ Tape directions on a digital recorder, tablet or on a website. Allow the student to use ear buds to listen to the directions.

## Accommodating Format

- ➤ Allow students to dictate answers into a tape recorder or digital device.

- ➤ Allow students to circle an answer instead of writing it out, as in: True or False.

- ➤ Rather than crossing out information when modifying a test, consider cutting and pasting or using white out, so that the test is less confusing. Make the test look visually "neat."

- ➤ Provide a checklist for essays.

- ➤ Give the student with "extra time" accommodation needs the essay materials in advance so he can be prepared to write.

- ➤ For matching items, be sure the definitions are on the <u>left</u>, and vocabulary words are on the <u>right</u> hand side of the page.

- ➤ Use capital letters for choice answers (ABCD and not abcd – in lower case, some students confuse the "b" and the "d").

- ➤ Try not to use words that can be difficult to discriminate. (Hear vs. here may test spelling, but not understanding of the word.)

On page 183, there is a matching test written by a music teacher. This test is incorrectly constructed, which is a common mistake that even publishing companies sometimes make.

In the left hand column are terms, and the right hand column contains the definitions. Setting up the test this way increases the students' reading load. The way many students would approach this test would be to take each term from the left hand column, then read all of the definitions on the right until they find the correct answer. Then they would repeat the process for B, and so on. If the columns had been reversed, the student could read the definition, "note on a line," and then scan down the column of visuals until the correct match was found.

The right hand column should always be the smallest/shortest amount of material and if applicable, it should be in alphabetical order.

The second mistake with this test is that it is not good practice when writing tests to have more than eight matching items. This is true for all students, not just for students with disabilities.

The third mistake is that there should always be one additional answer; so if you have eight questions, there should be nine choices from which to choose. The reason is that if there is an even number of questions and choices, when the student gets one answer wrong, two answers are automatically wrong.

# Example of a Poorly Constructed
# Matching Test for a Music Class

1. 𝅘𝅥

2. barline

3. [whole note on staff]

4. staff

5. 𝄢

6. 𝅝

7. time signature

8. measure

9. 𝄞

10. leger line

11. 𝅗𝅥

12. [staff]

13. brace

14. [whole note on staff]

A. note on a line

B. curved line and straight line used to connect the grand staff

C. whole note (not on a staff)

D. double barline

E. 5 lines and 4 spaces used for writing music

F. treble clef

G. note in a space

H. quarter note

I. the distance between 2 barlines

J. bass clef

K. vertical lines that separate measures

L. half note

M. tells how many beats in each measure

N. tells you to play louder

O. small line used for writing notes above or below the staff

# Modifying Tests and Quizzes
## Type 2 Ideas

## Modifying structure

- ➤ Use Type 1 accommodations

- ➤ Eliminate or consolidate questions (based on sifting)

- ➤ Keep similar questions together (for example, all division questions are in one section, and fractions are in another. Do not mix them up .) This helps students who have issues with "switching" due to processing speed.

## Accommodating directions

- ➤ Use Type 1 accommodations

- ➤ Use simple sentences

- ➤ Identify and define key terms

- ➤ Reread a set of directions before the student takes a section

- ➤ Give the student alternate directions, (fill a graphic organizer instead of writing an essay, or only compare - not contrast)

## Accommodating format

- ➤ Use Type 1 accommodations

- ➤ Eliminate possible choices

- ➤ Provide a word bank for fill-ins

- ➤ Chunk matching into sections of 4-5 questions. Always have one more response choice than questions for multiple choice.

- ➤ Chunk material into sections of 5 questions, ask students to pick 4 to answer

- ➤ Allow students to use notes or a study guide.

- ➤ Allow open book tests with page number references.

- ➤ Provide an outline for essays. Allow students to use notes or study guides as memory aids, or perhaps they can bring in a 3 x 5 card with some information on it.

# Practicing Modifying Tests

Here are some sample directions that would pose difficulties for students with disabilities. Try modifying the directions on your own, and then see page 186 for further information.

## Directions

Using Type 1 and Type 2 ideas, try modifying the following test directions:

> *Mark the following items True or False on the Scantron. Use "A" for True and "B" for False. If "B", then correct the sentence to make it true on the line below the question. If the sentence is true, write "okay" for that answer.*

Type 1 accommodations:



See suggestions for accommodating and modifying these directions on pages 186.

Type 2 modifications:



> *Essay question: Answer the following question in a complete paragraph, keeping in mind the rules for good paragraph construction (5 pts). Contrast the platform of the two candidates for governor. Describe their major campaign strategies and how these strategies affect their chances for being elected. (40 pts).*

See suggestions for accommodating and modifying these directions on page 187.

Type 1 accommodations:



Type 2 modifications:

# Possible Modifications to the Directions

*Mark the following items True or False on the Scantron. Use "A" for True and "B" for False. If "B", then correct the sentence to make it true on the line below the question. If the sentence is true, write "okay" for that answer.*

In this example, there are too many directions for a student with disabilities to follow. They are being asked to mark true or false, to remember to use A or B, to correct the sentence, and if it is already correct, to write "okay." One solution might be to separate out the request to correct the sentence and put it in another place on the test. Otherwise, there is too much processing required.

One way to modify these directions for a Type 1 student would be:

> ➤ Read each question
> ➤ Write out True or False next to the question
> ➤ (Value: 3 points each)

It's a good idea to put point values at the end of every section of the test, so that students can make an informed decision about what section of the test to take first. On a test, the essay tends to be located at the end, but it is also usually worth the most weight. A student might start on section 1 and spend a long time, then move onto section 2 and again spend a long time, get through sections 3 and 4, then try to cram in the essay at the end. Out of time, the student writes a very poor essay and fails the test. Students need to be taught that they can start where the points are heaviest and work backwards, which allows them to leave the lightweight material for the end when they're short on time. Many students don't know that they can take the test out of order and focus attention on the part that is worth the most points.

The Scantron is problematic for students with disabilities. The multiple choice answers on a Scantron are lettered A, B, C, D. Unfortunately, the two letters that dyslexics switch the most are B and D. Also, the Scantron lines are skinny, which poses a problem for students with visual tracking issues: they mark the answer in the wrong spot. Other students have trouble filling in the bubble. They write outside the borders and the computer reads it incorrectly and marks it wrong.

For a Type 2 modification, you might provide the words True and False after each question so that the student is only required to circle the word, rather than write it out. The modified directions would read like this:

> ➤ Read each question
> ➤ Circle "True" or "False" next to each question
> ➤ (Value: 1 pt each)

Another way to modify a test is to vary the weighting of various sections. In this case, you might reduce the point value from 3 points each to 1 point apiece.

Let's look at the second question on page 185:

*Essay question: Answer the following question in a complete paragraph, keeping in mind the rules for good paragraph construction (5 pts). Contrast the platform of the two candidates for governor. Describe their major campaign strategies and how these strategies affect their chances for being elected. (40 pts).*

Students do better when information is presented to them in a vertical format. So for a Type 1 accommodation, we might give the instructions in outline form, rather than in a horizontal prose format. The student can use the outline format as a checklist. Another modification would be to put little boxes by each section, so the student can go back and check off each box as sections are completed.

Essay question: (40 pts)

➢ Contrast the platform of the two candidates for governor.
➢ Describe their major campaign strategies.
➢ Describe how these strategies affect their chances for being elected.

Extra points: (5 pts)

➢ Write a complete paragraph to answer the essay question.
➢ Keep in mind the rules for good paragraph construction.

To create Type 2 modifications, first ask yourself what the test is for. If the purpose is to demonstrate that the student knows the material, an essay is not the best test. In that case, have him fill out a graphic organizer, such as the one below. If you need to find out whether the student is competent at writing an essay, then assign a familiar topic rather than new information. Otherwise, you're asking the student to accomplish two things simultaneously, which may pose difficulties.

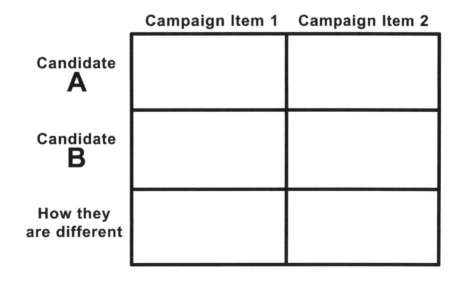

# Practicing Modifying Tests

## Structure and Format

Using Type 1 and Type 2 accommodation and modification techniques, modify the following samples for structure and format. Try the exercises on your own before looking at the suggestions on page 189. There's no one right or wrong way to create these modifications – it all depends on what works for your students.

1.  **WHICH OF THE FOLLOWING DOES NOT BELONG IN THE GROUP? WHY? (EXPLAIN BELOW)**

    **A. Freeport Doctrine**

    **B. fugitive slave act**

    **C. Dred Scott Decision**

    **D. Kansas-Nebraska Act**

    **E. a & b**

2.  On the line at the left, fill in the blank with the correct answer for all 25 questions.

    _____ 1. Holden leaves Pency a few days early to go to ___.

    _____ 2. Holden gets into a fight with _____ over his date
    With Jane Gallagher.

    _____ 3. Holden is ostracized by the fencing team because he - - - - - - - - .

3.  Match the term with the definition by placing the correct letter of the definition on the line next to the vocabulary word.

    | | | |
    |---|---|---|
    | _____ 1. Modify | A. Adapted to teach, instructive |
    | _____ 2. Didactic | B. To qualify, to change, to vary |
    | _____ 3. Teach | C. To instruct, to inform, to make familiar with |
    | _____ 4. Test | D. Petulant, peevish |
    | _____ 5. Testy | E. To bear witness to, to give evidence |
    | _____ 6. Testify | F. To put to a trial, to refine |
    | _____ 7. Testimonial | G. A gift in token of appreciation |

For the first question on page 188, what changes would you make? Here are some ideas:

➢ Use a more readable font. Do not use all capital letters.

➢ Limit the number of choices to two or three.

➢ The answer at "B" is not capitalized. Make it consistent by capitalizing "Fugitive" – otherwise, the student might think the lower case letter is a clue.

➢ Change "E. a & b" to "E. Freeport Doctrine and Fugitive slave act". Otherwise, the student has to process what "A" is, then what "B" is, and then what "A" and "B" are in combination. Writing them out makes it easier for processing purposes.

➢ Choose better wording: "Which of the following is different?" or "Which is not part of the group?"

➢ Students with disabilities have trouble following a long line of directions. A better option might be to turn it into a bulleted list.

➢ Remove the "Why?" and put it someplace else on the test as a separate question that requires a short answer.

➢ Change the question totally. Instead of a multiple choice question, turn this into an essay question: "Give one fact about the Freeport Doctrine or one fact about the Dred Scott Decision." Multiple choice only requires recognition, not interpretation. If you want to test students' ability to synthesize knowledge and have them practice higher order thinking skills, an essay question may be the preferable format. Otherwise, you risk simplifying the test until it's only knowledge and comprehension questions.

Let's take a look at the second question. Here are some ideas for modifications:

➢ Change the font so that it's easier to read. Many students with disabilities struggle with reading cursive writing.

➢ Change the spacing on the underlines so that they're a uniform length.

➢ Provide a word bank on 3 x 5" cards that the student can refer to.

➢ Put the question in kid-friendly language. Identify the referenced text within the question.

➢ Depending on the level of student or the type of modification, you might put possible answers up at the top to choose from.

➢ Choose a word other than "ostracize" (or define it).

- ➢ Replace dashes with blanks so that students don't try to find words with letters to fit the dashes. Example: _ _ _ _ (four dashes). Students may think you require a four-letter word.

- ➢ Although the blanks at left make it easier for teachers to correct the tests, two blanks can be confusing. Eliminate the blanks at the left, so that there is only one blank to fill in.

- ➢ Leave white space between the questions so that students have more room to write their answers.

Possible changes for question #3:

- ➢ Put the definitions in a column on the left side and put the shorter answers in the right hand column. (This reduces the amount of reading required.)

- ➢ Fix the alignment of the definitions so that they're easy to read.

- ➢ It might help to put the definitions in alphabetical order.

- ➢ The vocabulary words "test, testy, testify, testimonial" sound too much alike and seem designed to trick students, rather than assess what they know. Sift the curriculum to determine what things a student needs to know and which of these words can be replaced.

- ➢ There should be one more answer than there are questions.

There is no right or wrong way to assess and modify tests and quizzes. However, adhering to best practices, along with a dose of compassion and common sense, will allow you to see the test through the eyes of your struggling learners and help you modify accordingly.

# Alternative Assessments

Although we need our students to practice for high-stakes tests, the best way to do that is not always by way of a pencil and paper test. When designing a test from which a grade is derived, you may be able to tap into your students' intelligence area and have them create a project to demonstrate competency.

Type 3 and 4 modifications especially require alternative assessments, which are different ways of finding out what the student knows. Here are some alternative assessments a student can be given in lieu of a traditional test or quiz that can provide a student with opportunities to demonstrate competence:

- Portfolio assessments
- Create a poster
- Make a children's book
- Write a speech
- Design a class worksheet
- Create a class quiz
- Act out a scene
- Cook a food
- Write a song
- Perform a rap
- Write a poem and present it to class
- Sing, dance or act out the poem
- Job shadow and report in class how the information is used in everyday life
- Create a model
- Create a puzzle or a game like "Clue" for the class

# Grading FAQs

## Are there any laws about grading students with disabilities?

Grading students with modifications is at the discretion of the teacher and the student's Individualized Education Planning (IEP) team. Some court cases on this issue have identified two specific areas to consider:

➢ "In spite of" the child's disability, is the child otherwise qualified when given reasonable accommodations (Type 1 and some Type 2 modifications)?; or

➢ "Because of" the child's disability, do you tend to grade in a certain way?

If the child is achieving the general objectives of the course when given reasonable accommodations, then modified grading may not be necessary or appropriate. If you generally grade a certain way for all students with disabilities *(ipse dixit)*, then you need to question whether this is an appropriate practice or not. If you modify grades based solely on the fact the student has an IEP, then this may be construed as a discriminatory practice.

> Cases to look at:
> - Southeastern v. Davis
> - Alexander v. Choate
> - Ottawa (IL) Office of Civil Rights (grading variances)

## Who receives modifications?

In addition to students with disabilities, you might modify for at-risk learners, for students who don't have English as their first language, or even for the gifted. For students with gifts and talents, we modify by enriching and instructing them beyond the curriculum. Curriculum compacting can be considered a "modification." Therefore, just because a student receives modifications, it does not automatically justify modified grading practices.

## What about putting "modified" on a report card?

The literature and many professionals suggest the following: it may be an acceptable practice to put "modified" on a report card as long as:

1. You use it for <u>any</u> student who receives any type of modification, not just a particular group of students, such as students with disabilities.

2. It only goes on the report card and <u>not</u> on a transcript.

3. It is never labeled "modified as per IEP" or anything that breaches confidentiality rules.

4. It is discussed at the IEP meeting.

Always remember that the report card goes into the cumulative file, which is not the same as a confidential file. Writing "modified as per IEP" on anything in the cumulative file would be an indication that the student has a disability, therefore breaching confidentiality.

SAT administrators used to put stars next to students' SAT scores when they were taken with the untimed administration. However, they ran into a little bit of trouble because the stars indicated that the students had an IEP. Since the only students that were allowed to take the tests untimed were students with IEPs, their actions constituted a breach of confidentiality. For the same reason that you wouldn't place a star next to an SAT score, or "modified as per IEP" on a report card, you wouldn't write "Special Education Math" on a report card either, because that document resides in a cume file.

When developing a policy, check with your school and district-wide administration, as well as counsel, to ensure that the policy is not discriminatory.

**Sample policy:** *"It should be the policy of this school to employ differential standards for grading and course requirements. The regular classroom teacher is encouraged to modify the curriculum, instructional approaches, and grading practices for those identified as students with disabilities in the regular classroom."*

**Sample staff guideline:** *"...The difference between a modification and an accommodation must be made clear to students and parents at the IEP meeting. A modification is a change to the curriculum objectives: less content is expected to be mastered by the student. Generally, less written work is expected to be completed. Modifications must be asterisked on the report card for any student receiving a modification (even students without an IEP on file). Accommodations are strategies that allow students access to the curriculum. They are aids certain students need to help them learn the same material the rest of the class is learning. Oral tests, additional time, repeated directions, and pre-teaching are some examples. Accommodations are explained to the parents, documented on the IEP or 504 plan, but do not have to be asterisked on the report card."*

**Sample staff guideline:** *"Students that receive modifications that change the objectives of the curriculum will be given a grade based on their IEP or 504 plan outcomes. The course will have a "7" at the end of the number. For example: Humanities, section 3, will be for students receiving regular credit and weight. Humanities 37 will be for students who have been programmed (through an IEP) to receive alternate credit. This credit will be weighted differently for class ranking purposes."*

### What should I say to other students or to the parents of children without disabilities who may ask about modified practices?

If a parent asks you about another child (other than their own), you have the legal obligation to not divulge information (the obligation to maintain confidentiality). Therefore, you can only answer questions about their child. You might let them know that you differentiate your practice to ensure that each child receives appropriate instruction for their level based on your data. A parent always want their child appropriately challenged. Approached from this angle, most parents understand. If not, you may need to enlist the help of a supervisor or administrator. Remember that you are bound to keep certain information confidential.

## What about honor roll and diplomas?

Ask yourself these questions: "What is a diploma for? How about honor roll? What does it represent? Who should be entitled? If a student completes what you ask them to do and makes good grades, is that student entitled? Do high school diplomas look any different for your #1 student than for your #331 student? Did those students complete the same requirements? (Some schools and states have varying degrees of diplomas that address this issue.)

The National Honor Society is a recognition program for outstanding students in grades 10-12, with chapters in all 50 states. Membership is based on academic merit, and one of the requirements for many chapters is that students achieve a certain class rank. If students with disabilities achieve the prerequisites for honor roll or graduation, then they're entitled to that status, regardless of their overall ability relative to general education students.

## What about weighted grades?

Imagine this scenario: a general education student receives a B. In order to earn that B, he completed every assignment and took every test. Another student received modified tests, did not complete every assignment, did not answer all the questions, and yet he also received a B. One suggestion to correct the imbalance is that at the high school level, you might want to unweight that grade, so that the two B grades don't mean the same thing. On the other hand, if the student is receiving Type 1 accommodations, there is no need to consider alternative grading measures.

If a student consistently receives Type 2 modifications, and the student is completing about 70% of the curriculum, I would ask you to consider this: what percentage is your cutoff for students to receive a passing grade in your class? Can a student learn 60% of the curriculum or earn a D-minus and still get credit for your course? If so, then holding a student accountable for 70% of the curriculum should entitle that student to receive credit for the course.

## What about weighted classes?

Many classes are assigned a different "weight" or value than a general education course, such as advanced placement, honors, college prep courses, and special education. For students who take those classes, the grade point average (GPA) is determined and then it is weighted according to the type of class. The more weight a course carries, the higher up it can move a student in class rank. So if you unweight a course, you take that out of the equation.

# Grading FAQ's continued

Weighted rank is more of an issue at the high school level than it is at the middle school. If you're in a middle school and you don't have weighted courses, then you can retitle courses for students who are only learning a percentage of the curriculum—but be careful how classes are identified on transcripts. "Special education math" is inappropriate for a transcript; "Essentials of math" is a good substitute. The titles you want to stay away from contain the words "special education." Instead, title modified courses with names such as Fundamentals of Math, Basic Math, Elementary Biology, etc.

## What about college or the employer?

I once completed a research project on the subject of weighted grades and how they affect the admissions process at universities. In discussions with admissions officers at 50 different colleges, I discovered that colleges have numerous ways for screening applicants, including SATs, teacher recommendations and entrance exams. The transcripts are just one small part of the evaluation.

Students with disabilities can choose not to identify their disability in college or on the job. If they choose to identify, they are entitled to certain modifications and protections under section 504 and the Americans with Disabilities Act.

## Where can I find more information?

Check with your school council for more information regarding local laws, and policies related to grading students with disabilities.

Here are a few helpful publications and websites:

Legal Resource Publications offers a book based on case law, written by an attorney: *What Do I Do When...® The Answer Book on Assessing, Testing and Graduating Students with Disabilities -- Second Edition.*
You can find it by searching for product 300111 at: http://www.ShopLRP.com

The Council for Exceptional Children (http://www.cec.sped.org) offers answers to frequently asked questions. On their website, use the search term "grading students with disabilities".

The Association for Supervision and Curriculum Development (http://www.ascd.org) has an article that may be helpful. Search for: "Grading Exceptional Learners".

The Iowa Department of Education maintains a free website with answers to some frequently asked questions related to grading (http://EducateIowa.gov). Click on the "A to Z Index" tab, and then look for "Grades, Diplomas and Transcripts for Students with Disabilities"

# Alternative Grading Ideas

- Checklists

- Performance Based Learning Assessment (see page 197)

- Portfolio Summary / IEP grading (see pages 198-202)

- Portfolio

- Audit

- Pass/Fail

- Contract Grade

- Multiple Grades

- Shared Grades

- Rubric Grading

- Strategy List

- Narrative

- Pre/post test (% increase based on selected skills)

# PBLA's
## (Performance Based Learning Assessments)

These assessments can be easily modified by changing part of the task or by varying the point value of various items. In the example below, students were given an outline of what they needed to perform, and the point value for each element. Modifications can be easily made by changing the element or the point value. Students with disabilities can still earn a grade, but now we can clearly see what the student was held accountable to.

## Assessment List for <u>ROMEO & JULIET</u> paper

| Element | Point Value | Self Eval. | Teacher Eval. |
|---|---|---|---|
| The content of the article is accurate. | 20 | | |
| The article is written with a specific purpose in mind. | 10 | | |
| The article is well organized. It has a beginning, middle and end. | 20 | | |
| The article is informative. | 10 | | |
| Spelling and punctuation are correct. | 15 | | |
| Grammar and sentence structure are okay. | 15 | | |
| The article is presented neatly. | 10 | | |

## Modification ideas

| Element | Point Value | Self Eval. | Teacher Eval. |
|---|---|---|---|
| The content of the article is accurate. | 20 | | |
| The article is written with a specific purpose in mind. | 15 | | |
| The article is well organized. It has a beginning, middle and end. | 15 | | |
| The article is informative. | 10 | | |
| Spelling and punctuation are correct. | 5 | | |
| Grammar and sentence structure are okay. | 15 | | |
| The article is presented neatly. | 10 | | |
| The student had a writing conference with draft 2 | 10 | | |

# Portfolio Summaries *

On pages 199-202, you will see examples of Portfolio Summaries. Use these rubrics to translate an IEP into a letter grade. They simplify the task of modifications, both for content and for grading purposes. At the end of the quarter, these summaries are attached to the IEP for parental review. There is no question what the modified grade means when there is such clear documentation and proof.

To create a Portfolio Summary:

> Look at the curriculum standard and determine what it is that students need to learn for that grade.

> At the beginning of the school year, work with the general education teacher to determine what percentage of the content you will hold the student accountable to.

> Make a list of academic elements that the student will be expected to master.

> Depending on how much of the content the student will be learning, there is a rating of 1, 2 or 3. The key on the bottom of the Portfolio Summary explains what those numbers mean. Rate the student in each area of mastery. These ratings correlate to the measurement on the IEP goals.

> Be sure to rate the students for self-initiated or teacher-assisted learning. Some students can perform at the 100% level if the teacher is within an effective proximity, but as soon as the teacher steps away, the student can no longer independently complete the task. Self-initiation is a higher form of mastery.

To determine a modified grade:

> For each class, work with the teacher to devise a grading scale.

> At the end of the marking period, count up all the 1s, 2s and 3s, then divide the total by how many elements there are. (Calculating a mathematical average of all of the elements.)

> Depending on the scale that has been devised, the average will correspond with a letter grade. For instance, a 1.7 might equal a B+. With all of the skills that the child learned clearly delineated, and with a notation as to whether the child could work independently, there will be no question how the teacher arrived at the modified grade.

Place a clean copy of each summary in your modification file so that you're not reinventing the wheel every year. As the standards change or as the student masters an objective, the summaries can be tweaked so that they remain current.

*Portfolio summaries should be discussed with parents at the outset of the school year. They are predominantly used for students receiving extensive modifications who are not working on grade level standards.*

Portfolio Summary of <u>Language Arts</u>         Marking Period     1    

<u>Written Expression:</u>

| | | | | |
|---|---|---|---|---|
| * paragraph writing (overall) | 1 | 2 | 3 | TA/SI |
| -indents to start a paragraph | 1 | 2 | 3 | TA/SI |
| -writes 4-5 related sentences per paragraph | 1 | 2 | 3 | TA/SI |
| -avoids repetition of words and ideas | 1 | 2 | 3 | TA/SI |
| -writes content relating to the topic of the writing prompt | 1 | 2 | 3 | TA/SI |

<u>Literature:</u>

| | | | | |
|---|---|---|---|---|
| * answers 5 questions about the main idea of a story | 1 | 2 | 3 | TA/SI |
| * provides 2 important facts about each main character of a story | 1 | 2 | 3 | TA/SI |
| * describes the time and place of the story | 1 | 2 | 3 | TA/SI |
| * states the conclusion of a story | 1 | 2 | 3 | TA/SI |
| * predicts what might happen after the end of the story | 1 | 2 | 3 | TA/SI |
| * gives an opinion about the story, supported by three reasons | 1 | 2 | 3 | TA/SI |
| * makes a recommendation of the story/book to another reader by rating the material and explaining the reason for the rating | 1 | 2 | 3 | TA/SI |

<u>Grammar, Spelling and Vocabulary</u>

| | | | | |
|---|---|---|---|---|
| * capitalizes the beginning word in sentences | 1 | 2 | 3 | TA/SI |
| * punctuates the end of sentences | 1 | 2 | 3 | TA/SI |
| * spells 10 – 15 target words from <u>Wordskills</u> | 1 | 2 | 3 | TA/SI |
| * learns/reviews 10 – 15 target word meanings | 1 | 2 | 3 | TA/SI |
| *practices vocabulary activities through: | | | | |
| -synonyms exercises | 1 | 2 | 3 | TA/SI |
| -antonyms exercises | 1 | 2 | 3 | TA/SI |
| -multiple meanings | 1 | 2 | 3 | TA/SI |
| -related meanings | 1 | 2 | 3 | TA/SI |
| -meanings from context | 1 | 2 | 3 | TA/SI |

IEP Key:

1 = 70 – 100%     2 = 70 – 50%     3 = below 50%
SI = self initiated     TA = with teacher assistance

Portfolio Summary of <u>Computer Literacy</u>                Marking Period _____1_____

| | | | | |
|---|---|---|---|---|
| * shows skill to log on/log off the computer network (100% competency) | 1 | 2 | 3 | TA/SI |
| * shows skill to set the printer and print out documents | 1 | 2 | 3 | TA/SI |
| * completes open-ended statements using word processing skills | 1 | 2 | 3 | TA/SI |
| * completes answers to questions using word processing skills | 1 | 2 | 3 | TA/SI |
| * edits word processing papers of one page or less | 1 | 2 | 3 | TA/SI |
| * copies sentences from a prompt (80% competency) | 1 | 2 | 3 | TA/SI |
| * uses highlighting and boldface on copied sentences (80% competency) | 1 | 2 | 3 | TA/SI |
| * completes an objective quiz at 80% competency | 1 | 2 | 3 | TA/SI |
| * completes 6/12 word processing assignments in a marking period | 1 | 2 | 3 | TA/SI |

IEP Key:

1 = 70 – 100%        2 = 70 – 50%        3 = below 50%
SI = self initiated              TA = with teacher assistance

Portfolio Summary of <u>Geography</u>                    Marking Period _____1_____

| | | | | |
|---|---|---|---|---|
| * uses an atlas index to locate information | 1 | 2 | 3 | TA/SI |
| * identifies place names | 1 | 2 | 3 | TA/SI |
| * transfers place names to a blank map | 1 | 2 | 3 | TA/SI |
| * learns basic cultures of countries by locating facts in the textbook | 1 | 2 | 3 | TA/SI |
| * writes one piece of information about religion and politics for that culture | 1 | 2 | 3 | TA/SI |
| * writes a description of family life, including three facts | 1 | 2 | 3 | TA/SI |
| * does one oral presentation and/or project per cultural study as modified by the teacher | 1 | 2 | 3 | TA/SI |
| * completes mini-project as modified by teacher | 1 | 2 | 3 | TA/SI |
| * participates in group work as directed by teacher | 1 | 2 | 3 | TA/SI |
| * keeps geography dictionary organized in her notebook | 1 | 2 | 3 | TA/SI |

IEP Key:

1 = 70 – 100%          2 = 70 – 50%          3 = below 50%
SI = self initiated                TA = with teacher assistance

Portfolio Summary of __Math__                                    Marking Period __1__

| | 1 | 2 | 3 | TA/SI |
|---|---|---|---|---|
| * demonstrates accuracy using the calculator for math problem solving | 1 | 2 | 3 | TA/SI |
| * demonstrates accuracy in whole number operations (+, -, x, ÷) | 1 | 2 | 3 | TA/SI |
| * shows knowledge of fractions using visuals and/or manipulatives | 1 | 2 | 3 | TA/SI |
| * shows ability to write decimal amounts from whole number operations (+, -, x, ÷) | 1 | 2 | 3 | TA/SI |
| * understands 2-place decimal value of money by fraction counting and/or fraction amounts | 1 | 2 | 3 | TA/SI |
| * demonstrates ability to solve 1-step problems by explaining solution | 1 | 2 | 3 | TA/SI |
| * demonstrates knowledge of measurement (clock, ruler, liquid, dry) | 1 | 2 | 3 | TA/SI |
| * shows ability to count money to $1, $5, $10, $25, $50, $75, $100 | 1 | 2 | 3 | TA/SI |
| * can make change to $10, $20, $50, $70, $100 | 1 | 2 | 3 | TA/SI |
| * given two products can make the best consumer choice and explain why | 1 | 2 | 3 | TA/SI |
| * budgets money: given a certain total for shopping, paying bills and planning a trip or vacation | 1 | 2 | 3 | TA/SI |
| * can figure food costs and unit prices through computation and problem solving | 1 | 2 | 3 | TA/SI |

IEP Key

1 = 70 – 100%        2 = 70 – 50%        3 = below 50%
SI = self initiated              TA = with teacher assistance

## Do The Best With What You Have

Do you remember the colorful handkerchief from this book's introduction? It could be used in all kinds of ways, from mopping a brow to teaching geometric shapes. Here's another way it was used as a learning device by my former student, Daniel, who was my inspiration to write this book. As you may remember, Daniel worked hard to earn his high school diploma and graduated from college, despite his learning disability.

While Daniel was in college, I was coaching a girl's Challenger Baseball League, which is a type of Little League for kids with disabilities. Our team had a problem. During practice, not one of my athletes had been able to hit the ball – not even once. The season was about to start, and we were literally batting zero.

I called Daniel, who was a great athlete. He may have needed modifications in his academic work, but if you put a ball or a bat in his hand, he could accomplish miracles. So I asked him if he would come by while he was home for spring break and see if he could give the team and me some pointers.

Daniel watched us practice for a moment and instantly saw what the problem was. "I'll be right back," he said. When he returned, he had a handkerchief and a roll of duct tape. He squished the handkerchief into a ball and taped it up so that the ball was now a larger target.

"Here you go, Mrs. Kunkel. I think this ought to solve your problem."

"Daniel, that's a great modification. And here I am, a special education teacher, and I didn't even think of that."

"Don't you remember what you always told me?" said Daniel. "It's not important that you look at things for what they were meant to be. It's important that you do the best you can with what you have."

RESOURCES

# Selected Bibliography

For additional copies of this text, or for Sonya Kunkel's newest books on
co-teaching and other teaching strategies, please see www.KunkelConsultingServices.com

## Co-Teaching Text

**Benninghof, Anne M.**, *Co-Teaching That Works*, Jossey-Bass, San Francisco, CA 2012

**Friend, Marilyn and Lynne Cook.** *Interactions: Collaboration skills for school professionals, 4th ed.* Boston, ME: Allyn and Bacon, 2003.

**Kunkel, Sonya Heineman,** *Advancing your Co-Teaching Practices to Raise Student Achievement: a Value Added Instructional Intervention,* Kunkel Consulting Services, **www.kunkelconsultingservices.com**, 2011

**Murawski, Wendy W.**, *Collaborative Teaching in Secondary Schools, Making the Co-teaching Marriage Work!,* Corwin Publications: A Sage Company, California, 2009

**Reeves, Douglas B.**, *Leading Change in Your School: How to Conquer Myths, Build Commitment and Get Results,* ASCD, Alexandria, VA, 2009

**Robb Laura, et. al.,** *Reader's Handbook, A Student's Guide for Reading and Learning*, Great Source, Wilmington, MA

**Villa, Richard A. et al.** *A Guide to co-teaching: Practical tips for facilitating student learning.* Thousand Oaks, CA: Corwin Press, 2004.

**Walther-Thomas, Chriss,** Lori Korinek, Virginia L. McLaughlin, Brenda Toler Williams, *Collaboration for Inclusive Education, Developing Successful Programs*, Allyn and Bacon, Boston, 2000.

## Teaching and Learning Tools Text

**Boyles, Nancy N.**, *That's a GREAT Answer! Teaching Literature Response to K-3, ELL and Struggling Readers,* Maupin House, Gainesville, FL, 2007

**Byrd, Daphne, Polly Westfall,** *Guided Reading Coaching Tool, 1-6,* Crystal Springs Books, NH, 2009

**Diller, Debbie,** *Literacy Work Stations,* Stenhouse Publications, Portland, Maine, 2003

**Frei, Shelly**, Teaching Mathematics Today, Shell Education, Huntington Beach, CA, 2007

**Kartchner Clark, Sarah**, *Writing Strategies for Social Studies*, Shell Education, Huntington Beach, CA, 2007

**Kunkel, Sonya Heineman, and Margaret Rae MacDonald, Ph.D**. *The Path to Positive Classroom Management,* Kunkel Consulting Services, **www.kunkelconsultingservices.com**, 2012

**Kunkel, Sonya Heineman** *Simple and Powerful Teaching and Learning Strategies for Embedding Specially Designed Instruction in General Classrooms,"* Kunkel Consulting Services, **www.kunkelconsultingservices.com**, 2012

**Macceca, Stephanie**, *Reading Strategies for Science*, Shell Education, Huntington Beach, CA, 2007

**McAndrews, Stephanie,** *Diagnostic Literacy Assessments and Instructional Strategies, A Literacy Specialist's Resource*, International Reading Association, Newark, DE, 2008

**Silver, Harvey F., et. al.,** *So Each May Learn: Integrated Learning Styles and Multiple Intelligences*, ASCD, Alexandria, VA, 2000

**Silver, Harvey F., et al,** Tools *for Promoting Active, In-Depth Learning,* The Thoughtful Education Press, 2001

**Sliva, Julie A.**, *Teaching Inclusive Mathematics to Special Learners, K-6,* Corwin Press, Thousand Oaks, CA, 2004

**Tilton, Linda**, *The Teacher's Toolbox for Differentiating Instruction, 700 Strategies, Tips, Tools and Techniques*, Covington Cove Publications, Shorewood, MN, 2005

**Tomlinson, Carol Ann**, Caroline Cunningham Eidson, *Differentiation in Practice: A Resource Guide For Differentiating Curriculum, Grades 5-9,* ASCD, Alexandria, VA, 2003

**Vaughn, Sharon**, Sylvia Linan-Thompson, *Research-Based Methods of Reading Instruction Grades K-3,* ASCD, Alexandria, VA, 2004

## Videos

**Friend, Marilyn**, *The Power Of 2*, Forum on Education Production: second edition, 1996.

**Beninghof, Anne**, *Co-Teaching In Inclusive Classrooms, Part I (K-6)*, BER, Bellevue, WA, **www.ber.org**

**Beninghof, Anne**, *Co-Teaching In Inclusive Classrooms, Part II (K-6)*, BER, Bellevue, WA, **www.ber.org**

**Kunkel, Sonya Heineman**, *Practical Classroom Strategies for Making Inclusion Work, Grades 6-12*, BER, **www.ber.org** 2009

**Kunkel, Sonya Heineman**, *Using Co-teaching to Increase the Learning of All Students, Part I: Easy to Implement Strategies,* BER, Bellevue, WA, **www.ber.org**

**Kunkel, Sonya Heineman**, Using *Co-teaching to Increase the Learning of All Students, Part II: Strategies that Maximize the Instructional Impact of Inclusion Classrooms,* BER, Bellevue, WA **www.ber.org**

## Audio

**Beninghof, Anne**, *Co-Teaching That Works,* Effective Strategies for Working Together in Today's Inclusive Classrooms (Grades 1-12), BER, **www.ber.org**

**Kunkel, Sonya Heineman**, *Practical Classroom Strategies for Making Inclusion Work, (Grades 6-12)*, BER, Bellevue, WA, **www.ber.org**

## Websites

**Friend, Marilyn**, "The co-teaching connection", **http://www.marilynfriend.com/index.htm**

**Hibbard, Michael, et al.**, *Teacher's Guide to Performance-Based Learning and Assessment,* 1996, (publisher: ASCD) **http://www.ascd.org/publications/books/196021.aspx**

**Huggins, Marie, Jennifer Huyghe, and Elizabeth Iljkoski,** "Co-Teaching 101: Lessons from the Trenches", **http://www.cec.sped.org/**

"Keys to Effective Co-teaching Models: Needs Assessment and Program Planning", Developed for the Arkansas Department of Education, Co-teaching Professional Development Team, **University of Central Florida, http://arksped.k12.ar.us/documents/co_teaching/building_leadership_team_module.pdf**

**Lawton, Millicent**. "Co-teaching: Are two heads better than one in an Inclusion classroom? " *Harvard Education Letter* March/April 1999. 29 Aug. 2006 **http://www.edletter.org/past/issues/1999-ma/coteaching.shtml**

**Marston, Natalie.** "6 Steps to successful co-teaching." National Education Association. 2006. 29 Aug. 2006 **http://www.nea.org/teachexperience/spedk031113.html**

Tools for Teaching, **www.FredJones.com**

### A Few Response to Intervention Web Sites:

**www.interventioncentral.com** - A good starting point (many links)

**www.fcrr.org** - Florida Center for Reading Research

**www.chartdog.com** – Graphing and Charting

**www.easycbm.com** - Progress Monitoring Assessment Tools Reading and Mathematics

**www.rti4success.org** - Another good starting point


**For additional materials, including the new co-teaching APP
for android smart phones, as well as resources, coaching
or professional development opportunities,
contact Sonya Heineman Kunkel.
www.KunkelConsultingServices.com**

# Index

Made in the USA
Lexington, KY
28 February 2016